Helping Children Think about Bereavement

Each year, 3,000 children and young people between the ages of 1 and 19 die as a result of illness or accident. Around 5 per cent of children will have experienced the death of a parent by the time they are 16. Statistics indicate that up to 70 per cent of schools have a bereaved pupil in their care at any given time.

Helping Children Think about Bereavement provides a four-part differentiated story and activities to help normalise death and allow children to develop emotional literacy to talk about it. The author, along with Child Bereavement UK, has devised activities and guidance for teachers on how to use the story to develop children's emotional literacy and prepare them for bereavement, whether it affects them personally or through a friend's bereavement. This book also offers support for teachers and parents outlining how children's understanding of death develops and what can be helpful in supporting bereaved children.

The story is presented at different levels:

- for children aged 9–11
- for children aged 7–9
- for children aged 5–7
- for children who speak English as a second language
- for children in early years or with learning difficulties

Details surrounding death and its aftermath are not always readily talked about or well handled. When it does happen, children need to be able to express themselves and know that their feelings are a normal part of grieving. This book is an invaluable resource for all Key Stage 1 and 2 teachers, teaching assistants and anyone who is involved in bereavement training.

Heather Butler has over thirty years' experience teaching in primary classrooms and has worked with many children facing bereavement.

Helping Children Think about Bereavement

A differentiated story and
activities to help children
age 5–11 deal with loss

Heather Butler

Routledge
Taylor & Francis Group

LONDON AND NEW YORK

First published 2013
by Routledge
2 Park Square, Milton Park, Abingdon, Oxon OX14 4RN

Simultaneously published in the USA and Canada
by Routledge
711 Third Avenue, New York, NY 10017

Routledge is an imprint of the Taylor & Francis Group, an informa business

British Library Cataloguing in Publication Data
A catalogue record for this book is available from the British Library

Library of Congress Cataloging in Publication Data
Butler, Heather.
   Helping children think about bereavement: a differentiated story
   and activities to help children age 5–11 deal with loss/authored
   by Heather Butler.
   p. cm.
   1. Bereavement in children. 2. Grief in children. 3. Children and death.
   I. Title.
   BF723.G75B88 2013   155.9'37083 – dc23
   2012040266

ISBN: 978–0–415–53684–4 (hbk)
ISBN: 978–0–415–53685–1 (pbk)
ISBN: 978–0–203–11126–0 (ebk)

Typeset in Bembo
by Florence Production Ltd, Stoodleigh, Devon, UK

MIX
Paper from
responsible sources
FSC
www.fsc.org   FSC® C013056

Printed and bound in Great Britain by
TJ International Ltd, Padstow, Cornwall

Contents

Introduction

This resource is designed to be used by primary schools to start conversations and encourage learning around the emotive subjects of loss, death and dying.

The aim is that by taking a step-by-step approach, the sensitive and carefully planned activities will help children learn that death and dying is not something to be feared and that it is okay to talk about it.

Although not its primary aim, it can also be used as a support resource with children who have been bereaved.

It is essential that you read Chapter 1 and the Preparing section in Chapter 2 before beginning and also familiarise yourself with where other information can be found.

FROM THE AUTHOR

Having taught in UK primary schools for over thirty years, I am now working part time to allow space to write, lead story-writing workshops and lead INSET. See www.heatherbutler.info for more details.

I have taught several children whose worlds were turned upside down when someone important to them died. Although I did my best, like many teachers facing this situation, I felt unprepared and inadequate.

The primary aim of the book is to equip children, and the adults who work with them, with language so they can talk about feelings, emotions and behaviours associated with bereavement. It is primarily a 'before it happens' book; it could also be used as a means of opening up difficult conversations following a death.

Children who view dying and death as something natural, and have the emotional literacy to be comfortable talking about it, will handle bereavement differently from those who do not.

The story of Marasova originated when I was teaching full time. One of my Year Fives was seriously ill so, as a class, we created a story and a pop-up book to send to him. Unbeknown to the children, the story had two endings. The class knew the happy ending where the turtle was painted bright yellow. Thankfully, I never needed the other ending where the turtle died.

The story then lay dormant for ten years until the opportunity came to work in partnership with Child Bereavement UK to create this resource. Child Bereavement UK is the UK's leading national organisation that supports families and educates professionals, when a baby or child of any age dies or is dying or when a child is facing bereavement. It trains around 5,000 professionals each year. The charity has been recognized as a quality provider of information to the public by the Information Standard, a Department of Health Scheme ensuring clear, accurate and up-to-date information.

It has been a privilege working with Child Bereavement UK, especially Jill Adams who is in charge of the Buckinghamshire Schools Support. She helped trial the lessons and worked on the support materials. Thank you for your words of wisdom and personal support as we worked on this project.

Dr Ann Rowland, Director of Bereavement Services at the charity, gave invaluable advice and guidance as the story developed and managed the project from Child Bereavement UK's point of view. Thank you for your patience, helpful comments, and all the time you have put in to reading various drafts of the story.

I would also like to thank Bruce Roberts and Hamish Baxter at Routledge for their support, the community at Manor Farm Junior School, Hazlemere, Bucks and, as always, my husband and family.

Thank you, too, to Tim Solosy who drew the illustrations. It has been good working with you.

Finally, a huge thank you to the following teachers who found time to road test the material after it was trialled and before it went for publication: Frankie Allen, Vasanti Pithia, Donna Spooner, Gemma Efford, Julia Richards, Sharon Bravington, Jo Miles and Sara Mason.

Important things to think about before you start

Child Bereavement UK
REBUILDING LIVES TOGETHER

www.childbereavementuk.org
Tel 01494 568900

LOOKING AFTER YOURSELF

Talking about bereavement and loss with children is emotionally draining. Feeling that you could do with some support is not an inability to cope, or of professional incompetence, but a recognition that everyone needs help sometimes.

We all have losses, big and small, which impact on our daily lives. This project may catch you unawares by stirring up emotions and feelings associated with previous losses. If it all feels too close to home, do not be afraid to say so. This is not a sign of weakness but merely recognising that we all have our limits.

It is perfectly normal and okay to be emotionally affected, and for the children to see that you are, but this needs to be done in a contained way.

Professional boundaries

When working in a school environment, it is easy to let the carer in us take over and forget our professional boundaries. Getting over involved is not helpful to either yourself or the children. Do take a caring and supportive approach but one that recognises your professional role. No matter how well meant or strong the desire to take the pain away, always try to be realistic with the amount of support that you can give. Providing a listening ear once a week, and sticking to it, is more meaningful than the offer of help anytime when inevitably that cannot be achieved in a busy school environment.

Don't forget that you can ring the Child Bereavement UK Support and Information Line 01494 568900 for a confidential chat, or just reassurance. Informal peer support in the staffroom can be a welcome opportunity to talk through issues and concerns and reduce feelings of inadequacy by sharing helping strategies.

LOOKING AFTER YOUR PUPILS

Children are naturally curious about how we might feel and what we do when someone dies. They are usually happy to talk about the end of life as long as this is done in a sensitive way and within a safe environment. It is adults who are hesitant, having acquired fears and anxieties around something that for many is still a subject they find hard to speak about – precisely what this project hopes to change. Provided with reassurance and support, most parents/carers will be receptive to their children taking part in the story. Sensitive and honest communication from school is the key to this. It is essential that parents are informed about the lessons (see suggested letter on page 6).

It is essential that some preparation work is done with your class before starting the story. As with adults, the activities may stir up feelings and emotions in some of the children and you need to have thought through beforehand how to respond. Consider who to go to should any 'tough stuff' be revealed, or child protection issues arise.

Also, identify where to go should you feel out of your depth. You can always call the Child Bereavement UK support and information line 01494 568900 or visit the website www.childbereavementuk.org for guidance and help.

Being aware of pupils who have experienced the death of someone they know, or even a family pet, is very important. The included sample letter to parents has a section requesting parents/carers to let you know of any deaths or other information that may impact on the class sessions.

Let any bereaved pupils know what you are proposing to cover in class and, if appropriate, give them the opportunity to opt out should they wish. Once every-thing is explained, most choose to stay in class and join in with everybody else.

In order to create a safe environment in the classroom, it is a good idea to have some ground rules. The ones suggested below are used at the beginning of every lesson in the story.

- You don't have to share something if you feel it is too private.
- Listen carefully to each other.
- After someone dies, some people feel very sad and other people might not feel anything at all. We're all different and it is okay not to feel the same as other people.

INFORMATION FOR PARENTS AND CARERS

The information on the following page can be given to parents and carers to help allay any fears. It will also help them to answer questions children may ask at home as a consequence of what they have been doing in class.

Guidance for Parents and Carers

Your child's teacher is delivering a programme of lessons which in a helpful and sensitive way encourages the class to think about, ask questions around, and learn about, feelings associated with loss, including loss through someone dying. Below is information that you may find helpful to answer any questions your child may have at home, and generally what approach to take if chatting with your child about what they have been doing in class.

How do I answer my child's questions?

Adults naturally want to protect, but children have a much greater capacity to deal with the realities of life than we realise, as long as they are spoken to in an appropriate way. Even a sad truth will be better than uncertainty and confusion. Questions are healthy, as is curiosity; so try to answer with simple, honest words. If you do not know what to say, contact the Child Bereavement UK support and information line 01494 568900 or have a look at the family section on their website www.childbereavementuk.org.

The word 'dead' feels harsh: should I use it?

Phrases such as 'gone to sleep' or 'passed away' or words such as 'lost' might feel kinder but are misleading and will lead to confusion and complication. The class activity encourages the children to use feelings words and language associated with the end of life in an honest way, and this includes the use of the word 'dead'. It is helpful if you can mirror this honesty at home. By doing so, your children will find it easier to share with you any situation they are finding difficult, such as issues with friends or being bullied at school.

Is it okay for children to see me upset?

The class activity might generate conversations with your child that result in you getting emotional or upset. Children need adults to be models, not heroes. Seeing adults expressing emotion can give a child of any age 'permission' to do the same, if they feel they want to. Don't be afraid to share your feelings; if adults are open and expressive, children are likely to be so too.

Child - Bereavement UK
REBUILDING LIVES TOGETHER

www.childbereavementuk.org Tel 01494 568900

2 The lessons

PREPARING

Read through Chapter 1: **Important things to think about before you start**.

Choose which version of the story is right for your class. Read it through and familiarise yourself with the activities. The script gives the wording for difficult questions and **TIPs** have been added after trialling the material.

Further preparation is minimal – mostly downloading pictures. If working with children who have learning difficulties, a shoe box beach will need making.

Children respond to the story and thoughts coming from it mostly by drawing or sharing ideas with a partner. Children need whiteboards or paper.

Ensure that you have informed parents/carers and that you are aware of any children for whom the story might be difficult.

SUGGESTED LETTER TO PARENTS/CARERS

Parents and carers need to be informed. The letter on page 6 explains what children will be learning about and asks for information so teachers know of children who might find the lessons difficult.

Dear Parents/Carers,

As part of developing children's emotional health and wellbeing, in PSHE we will be doing four sessions titled 'Helping children think about bereavement'. The resource material we will be using was written in partnership with Child Bereavement UK and is based on a story about a turtle. It covers a variety of emotions, including those associated with grief and bereavement.

The aim is to help children be aware of, and able to talk about, how they and others might feel if a pet, or someone they know, dies.

Inevitably, as they grow up, children experience different types of loss. If given the opportunity to learn about losses, big and small, in a sensitive and supportive way, they will be more able to cope. Children have a natural curiosity about the end of the life cycle and are usually happy to think about and discuss feelings associated with it.

To help prepare and plan the lessons, it is essential I know about any people, or pets, that might have been important to your child but are now no longer part of their lives. The sessions provide opportunities for children to share experiences if they wish to and being aware will help me respond in a supportive and helpful way. Any details will be treated sensitively.

Support material is also available for parents; please do contact me if you have any concerns, questions, or would like more information.

Child Bereavement UK has an excellent website

www.childbereavementuk.org

that you may be interested in, and also a support and information line on **01494 568900**.

Thank you.

STORY OUTLINE

There are four parts (lessons) in each version, the content of which is outlined below with key points in bold.

The first part introduces the characters and setting – Peter, Anji and their parents.

The children are feisty, real and argue with each other. Their house has cliffs and a private beach as part of their garden.

Marasova turtle arrives after a storm. The children understand what he says and he makes wishes when it is his birthday. He longs for his shell to be bright yellow.

In the second lesson Peter shows anger because he is not in the school football team.

Anji winds him up further. Later they lose Marasova and feel scared because they have no control over what is happening and fear Marasova has been dragged out to the big sea.

In the third lesson the children visit their grandmother. Returning home, Marasova is ill. Anji and Peter's lives still carry on. Living with someone who is ill can be difficult. After he recovers, Anji and Peter tiptoe to the beach at night to paint his shell while he is asleep. Anji then feels guilty because Mum and Dad do not know where they are. The gulls use Marasova's shell as target practice to dump poo on until the children put polish on it and the poo slides off. When snow falls Peter and Anji have a brilliant day on the beach with great memories.

In the final part, the little gull is injured. Marasova looks after him and befriends the other gulls. They form a community to care for each other. The children will need their community of friends when they find Marasova's cold body. Their immediate reactions are denial, tears, looking after each other and telling their parents.

For children aged 9–11

1 THE BEACH, THE CHILDREN AND THE TURTLE

Children think about special places, special people, feelings and wishes they make. Throughout, the term 'children' refers to those listening to and interacting with the story. The children in the text are referred to as Peter and Anji.

Preparation

Download pictures of (in this order) a) unpopulated beach, b) steps leading down a cliff face to a beach, c) blue and yellow dinghy, d) turtle.

Further pictures will be added each session.

■ Explain that this story is about feelings, including feelings we might have after someone has died. To help children feel safe, certain ground rules need to be talked about . . .

  1   You don't have to share something if you feel it is too private.
  2   Listen carefully to each other.
  3   After someone dies, some people feel very sad and other people might not feel anything at all. We're all different and it is okay not to feel the same as other people do.

These ground rules are really important and will be repeated at the beginning of every lesson to help children remember them.

> **TIP**
>
> Phrases and concepts needing careful wording or explanation are written so they can be used directly from the script. These are indicated by the word 'Say' or 'Ask' written on a line with the question or comment on the line below.

■ Look at a picture of an empty beach on the whiteboard. Ask children to think of one thing that could be added to the picture. Also look at pictures of a cliff with steps and a blue and yellow dinghy.

■ Ask children to divide a whiteboard or piece of paper into four and label each section 'Mum', 'Dad', 'Anji' and 'Peter'. As you read the first part of the story, ask children to jot down feelings the four characters experience in the appropriate box as the story is read.

Peter says, 'When they made these steps, did they start building at the top or the bottom?'

And Anji, who has never even thought about this before, says,

'It's obvious. You'd start at the top.'

And Peter says, 'No you wouldn't. You'd row round the cliffs with wood in a boat and start at the bottom.'

'If you knew the answer, why did you ask me?' Anji says.

And Peter says, 'Because I wanted to annoy you.'

He jumps off the bottom step and races towards Ed's shed. Before long, wet sand shoots out behind his bicycle wheels. He loves this beach more than anywhere in the world.

So does Anji. Today she wants to find some shells for Bob to look after. Bob lives in Granny's garden and doesn't say much. She only finds three before Dad and Mum appear at the top of the cliff.

'We've got the dinghy,' Dad yells.

'Shell Sea! Chel-sea!' Peter chants, steering his bike towards the steps.

'No way!' Anji shouts, running after him. 'The boat is not going to be called Chelsea. It is going to be called Sea . . . Shell.'

'Dad said it could be Shell Sea,' Peter shouts back.

'Well I am always going to call it Seashell,' Mum says, and Dad, who is three steps behind her, flares his nostrils in a most hideous way. So Anji tells him to stop doing it.

'How about if the boat has two names?' he says, 'the yellow part can be called Seashell and the blue part, Shell Sea.'

The inflatable dinghy is a present from Granny who is 65 today and a bit dippy. She always sends them a present to say 'thank you' for the one they send her.

Dad shows Anji and Peter how to use the foot pump and soon the dinghy is ready.

'You take the boat out first, with Anji,' he says to Mum. 'Peter and I have something special to do.'

'What are you up to?' Mum asks.

'Nothing,' Dad smiles.

Mum and Anji pull on the oars and the front of the boat cuts through the water. Having a beach as part of your garden is awesomely amazing. Having a boat as well is the best thing ever.

Until Mum suddenly points at the cliffs and says,

'Look what those two are doing! Anji, turn the boat round.'

■ Ask children what they think Dad and Peter are doing back on the beach.

'Have you come to tell us how much you like our beautiful blue goal post?' Dad calls out as Mum sweeps up the beach like a toy car with a brand new battery.

'You cannot paint on the cliff,' Mum says. 'You might be 38 but you are so irresponsible.'

'Don't explode too much or your brains will fall out,' Dad says. 'I bought paint that will wear off in a few months.'

'But . . . but . . .' Mum says.

Peter is standing next to Dad holding a huge paintbrush dripping with blue paint. He is giggling and Mum suddenly starts laughing too because the blue goal post lines are all wiggly and Dad and Peter think they have been so clever painting it while she and Anji are out of the way in the boat.

Anji joins in the laughing too because she knows that the beach and her family, even her little brother, who can sometimes be a pain in the neck, are so brilliantly special.

- Ask children if they would like to be part of the family, and why.

- On the left-hand side of the board, make a list of the feelings children have jotted down while the story was being read. Working with a partner, ask children to choose one feeling they are okay with (i.e., enjoy feeling) and one they are not so comfortable with. Tell their partner about when they have experienced these two feelings.

- Say,

  The beach is Anji and Peter's favourite place. Draw your favourite place and your favourite people. Share ideas with a partner.

TIP

Keep tasks short and sharp. Allow only a short time for drawing tasks – enough to record thoughts but not resemble an art lesson.

- While children are doing this, write these turtle dictionary words on the right-hand side of the board.

  cranthi – hello
  frillda – grey
  mumin – stupid
  spluff – seagull
  grilopsi – yellow
  yumgo – chocolate cupcake
  umpo – gull poo

- Ask children why they think the words have been written on the board. They will find out as the next part of the story is read.

Marasova arrives after a whoppingly scary storm.

'Cranthi,' he says in a deeply croaky voice when Anji and Peter first notice him. 'Pleased to meet you.' Peter and Anji do not expect a large turtle to be sitting next to Ed's shed, let alone one that talks; and the spookily weird thing is, they both understand him, even though he speaks his own language.

'That turtle just said "hello, pleased to meet you",' Peter whispers.

'I know,' Anji whispers back.

'Where have you come from?' Peter asks him.

'The Big Sea,' Marasova says. 'I like this beach. It's a lovely place for a turtle to live.'

'We'll have to make an adoption certificate for him,' Mum says when they tell her, 'to prove he belongs to us. He'll need a birthday as well.'

'And a chocolate birthday cake,' Dad says. He would eat chocolate cake all day if Mum let him.

October 1st is the next time the children go to the beach so that date becomes his official birthday.

'How old do you want to be?' Peter asks him.

'Nine. Then I am one year older than you and one year younger than your sister,' Marasova says.

So the children put nine candles on a yumgo.

'What is it?' Marasova says.

'A birthday cake, with one candle for every year,' Anji says.

'You blow out the candles and make a wish,' Peter adds.

So Marasova takes a deep breath.

'I wish . . .' he says, 'that my shell was grilopsi instead of frillda.'

'Shh! You're not supposed to tell anyone what you wish!' Anji says.

'It will never happen,' Marasova laughs. 'I'll always be frillda. Making a wish won't change that.'

'But you're meant to keep it a . . .' But Anji never finishes the sentence because a greedily squawking spluff suddenly swoops in, sticks its beak in swirly sugar icing and takes off again with half a chocolate yumgo hanging from its beak.

'Oy!' Peter shouts, 'give that back!' But the spluff circles in victory above them before dumping a splodge of sticky white poo. It lands two centimetres from Peter's left foot.

'Mumin spluff,' he shouts at it. 'You nearly hit me.' But all the spluff does is gracefully loop-the-loop then glide off towards the cliff tops.

On the way home Peter asks,

'Why don't you tell people what you wish when you blow out birthday cake candles?'

And Anji, who thinks she knows about these things, says,

'Because you might wish for something stupid.'

Peter climbs a few more steps then says,

'When Marasova wished he was grilopsi, that was a bit stupid, wasn't it? Because it could never happen.'

But Anji doesn't answer. It is Nina's birthday next week and she is deciding how many pots of pink nail varnish to buy her best friend for a present.

■ Ask children what, in the story, could and could not happen in real life.

> **TIP**
>
> Marasova does NOT morph into other things or do magic tricks. He talks and knows about Anji and Peter's life but is still semi-constrained by physical things a turtle can do.

■ Divide a whiteboard or piece of A4 paper into four. In each section ask children to write a different type of wish they have made.

 1 a regret *(I wish I hadn't done . . .)*
 2 a hope *(I wish something would happen . . .)*
 3 a ritual *(birthday cake wish, New Year resolution)*
 4 a wish that will never happen *(If only . . .)*

 Ask children to think about which feelings from the list on the left-hand side of the board go with each of these wishes. Share their thoughts with a partner.

■ Say,

> Today we have thought about feelings and wishes. Some feelings might have been happy ones, some sad. These are feelings everyone has and we are learning about them now; even when you get older you will still be learning about them.
>
> Wishes are important too; sometimes they can come true and sometimes they can't.

■ Let children draw anything they like from the story so far. This is to give them time to start processing what has been thought about during the lesson.

2 FOOTBALL TEAMS, BUILDING SANDCASTLES AND LOSING MARASOVA

Children think about their response to things they cannot control. One possible response is anger. They then think how they might feel when someone important to them has gone.

Preparation

Add pictures of building sandcastles and fighting the tide to previous ones.

- On whiteboards or paper, ask children to draw one thing they remember from the story last time. Share their pictures with the class to recap what happened in the story.

- Revisit the ground rules.

  1 You don't have to share something if you feel it is too private.
  2 Listen carefully to each other.
  3 After someone dies, some people feel very sad and other people might not feel anything at all. We're all different and it is okay not to feel the same as other people do.

- Say,

  Today we are thinking about when things happen that we cannot control and how that might make us feel. We're also going to think about how we might feel if someone or something that is important to us goes missing.

- Look at pictures of children building sandcastles and fighting the tide. Make sure children understand what these are.

  Then read the next part of the story.

Peter is really grumpy.

'Mr Hawkins only chooses tall people for the Year 4 football team,' he whinges. 'That's why I'm not in it.'

'Mmmm,' Marasova says. 'Go over there and dig a hole then stand back and chip the ball into it.'

So Peter digs a hole, tries to kick the ball into it and Marasova knows exactly why he has not been chosen for the school football team; he is completely hopeless. Marasova tells him to stand next to the hole.

'Surely you'll get it in now,' he says.

And he does.

'Tomorrow,' Marasova says gently, 'we will practise kicking the ball against the blue faded goal you and your dad painted on the cliff face.'

Anji, meanwhile, is sitting cross-legged on the sand next to Ed's shed surrounded by shells, decorating them with Mum's paints.

'Come and paint a shell,' she says when Marasova and Peter join her. 'Mine are all pink.'

Peter pulls a face like he thinks his sister is a brainless slug.

'I hate pink,' he says.

'Clever people like pink,' Anji says smugly, straightening her pink tee-shirt as she says it.

'No they don't,' Peter shouts. 'Pink's stupid.'

'Just because you're useless at football,' Anji jeers at him.

'Oi, stop it, you two,' Marasova says.

But they ignore him and carry on bickering even though Marasova hates it when they do that.

'The tide is coming in,' he says. 'We haven't built a sandcastle for ages. If we do that, will you two stop being horrible to each other?'

'Maybe,' Anji says.

'No,' Peter says.

The sandcastle they build is ginormously huge and when it is finished Peter lifts Marasova on top of it.

He stays there while waves slosh round the moat and chunks of sand crumble off the sides of the castle. Anji and Peter build dams and channels to try to stop the water reaching the castle. They know they will never win and when the castle finally collapses, Marasova swims out to sea leaving the children to flatten the mound of sand that is left, before the sea does.

'You're useless, aren't you?' Anji says as soon as Marasova has gone. She pushes him out of the way. 'You're just skinny and little and weak and . . .'

Peter throws himself at her legs. They both topple into the water.

'I'm not skinny and I'm not little,' he yells.

'Oh yes you are.'

'I'm not weak either.'

'You are,' Anji shouts, pushing him over again. 'And you are so pathetic you are probably going to cry,' she adds.

And Peter hurts inside because Amin and Dougie are in the football team that's playing in the cup next week and Peter isn't even a substitute. He turns away so his sister cannot see the tears in his eyes. High above them gulls squawk as if they are laughing at him because he is useless.

■ Ask children to draw a horizontal line on whiteboards or a piece of paper and write HAPPY on the left-hand side and ANGRY on the right. Now add several more feelings above the line. There is no right or wrong answer as to where the words should be written.

■ Think about how these feelings might make someone behave. Can children think of any actions that might go at either end? For example, punching in anger or punching the air in delight.

TIP

Use this as an opportunity to reinforce the idea that people see things differently.

■ Ask,

> Like Peter, when have you wanted to do something and not been able to?
>
> Draw it on whiteboards or paper.
>
> Write one of the feelings on the board to describe how you felt.
>
> Share ideas with a partner.

■ On the board underneath the HAPPY/ANGRY line, make a class list of ten things children cannot change or control – e.g. weather, the date of their birthday, death, the time of their favourite TV programme, having curly or straight hair.

■ Not being in control made Peter angry. How did it make him behave?

■ On whiteboards or paper, ask children to draw what they think of when you say the word . . . 'anger'. Draw for about two minutes, then share what children have drawn.

TIP

Encourage children to draw in silence.

■ Remind children they do not have to share anything they do not want to.

■ Ask,

> Have you ever taken your anger out on anyone else? What happened?
>
> Share answers with a partner.

16

- ■ Ask,

    How might you help yourself when you feel angry?

    Make a list of strategies on the board, underneath the HAPPY/ANGRY line.

- ■ Read the next part of the story.

Marasova loves riding in the dinghy. He sits at the front, humming happily to himself. Behind him, Peter and Anji sit side by side in their life jackets. They are rowing towards the orange markers that are there for safety; beyond them, they might be swept in to the Big Sea by the underwater currents.

Normally, Anji gets cross with Peter because he is not strong enough to pull on the oars like she can. But today he feels super-charged and manages to keep up with her. He is very pleased with himself and turns round to grin at Marasova.

Only the turtle is not there.

'He'll have gone for a swim,' Anji says, but Peter shakes his head.

'He always tells us if he is going for a swim,' he says. 'Do you think he has fallen off the boat and is trapped underneath it?'

'No,' Anji says in a big sister sort of way. 'And anyway, he can swim underwater.'

But Peter says,

'Where is he then?'

They both stare into the swirling water beneath them and as they do the tug of the current pulls them further away from the beach, beyond the orange markers, towards the Big Sea.

'Peter, we've got to row back,' Anji says.

'How strong are Marasova's legs?' he asks and there is a quiver of panic in his voice.

'He'll be all right,' Anji says quickly.

'Can turtles hold their breath for a long time?'

'Peter, stop talking and pull on the oars. Marasova will be all right.'

But Peter carries on,

'If Marasova was dragged out to the Big Sea, would Mum and Dad be able to find him?' and as he says this, his oar skids and he falls backwards making the dinghy nearly tip over.

'Oy! Watch out!' Anji shouts at him. 'You could have had us both in the water.'

'Well I didn't, did I?' Peter says and beneath them the sea is dark and dangerously deep.

'Just pull on the oar and row,' Anji says, wishing the orange markers would get closer. The currents are strong and the dinghy is still drifting out. 'If Marasova *has* gone, there's nothing we can do about it, is there?'

And she is right.

There isn't.

'Marasova's gone, hasn't he? Back to the Big Sea,' Peter says and he feels very, very small and a little bit scared.

Anji doesn't answer. She just keeps tugging at the oars and Peter does the same and it seems to take forever before they are back inside the orange markers.

At least she and Peter are now safe.

The gulls above wheel and turn and squawk as the children row back to the beach.

'We'd better tell Mum and Dad,' Anji says as they drag the dinghy on to the sand.

'Why did Marasova leave? Why did he want to go back to the Big Sea? Was it because of us?' Peter asks in a small voice. 'Was it because we argued with each other?'

'I don't know,' Anji says and she feels like she wants to cry.

And then a chuckling sort of voice behind her says, 'Great swim.'

Both children spin round and there he is, looking up at them with a big grin on his wrinkled face. And suddenly the sun is shining and everyone is smiling and Peter's ribcage starts to feel normal again.

■ Ask children to write a quick summary of how they would have felt if they had been Peter when he thought Marasova had gone. Have children ever felt like that themselves?

Share with a partner how they felt.

■ Ask children to think of a time when they were certain they knew where something was but when they looked it wasn't there. Draw what it was.

Share with a partner how they felt when they realised it had gone.

TIP

If children cannot think of anything, they can draw Peter and Anji realising Marasova was not in the boat.

- Say,

  > Today we have thought about how things happen and we cannot always control them. It might make us feel angry. It could also make us feel scared and helpless, especially if something or someone who is really important goes missing.

- Let children draw anything they like from the story to give them time to start processing what has been talked about.

3 SEVEN DAYS AND THEN MARASOVA IS PAINTED

Children think about grandparents, when someone is ill, what might make us feel guilty and the importance of memories.

Preparation

Add pictures of home-made biscuits. Find a picture of a grandparent wearing false teeth.

- To help children feel safe, certain ground rules need to be talked about.
  1. You don't have to share something if you feel it is too private.
  2. Listen carefully to each other.
  3. We all have feelings and we are all different and it is okay not to feel the same as other people do.

- Recap the story by looking at pictures from the previous two sessions and then at the biscuits and false teeth.

- Today we are thinking about grandparents, what happens when someone is ill and what might make us feel guilty.

- Now read the next part of the story.

At half term Anji and Peter visit Granny. They take decorated shells and pebbles for Bob to look after in her garden

'Does Bob support Chelsea?' Peter asks, patting the gnome's grinning blue head.

'Of course he does,' Granny says. 'Everyone in this house supports Chelsea.'

'I like Bob,' Peter says and pulls a face at Anji when Granny bends over to put a yellow shell next to Bob's right foot.

Granny helps them make biscuits, reads books to them and talks to Ed's photograph sitting on the television.

'I still miss him,' she says. 'I even miss his motorbike cluttering up the garage.'

The children miss their grandad too. He sent them emails, played football, read books and played cards with them.

'I wish he was still alive,' Peter says.

'So do I,' Granny says and sighs. 'But he's not, and I have to get on with what I'm doing, though sometimes that is really difficult.'

■ On whiteboards or paper, ask children to write or draw something they have done with their grandparents.

TIP

If children have never known their grandparents, let them draw pictures of things they have done with another relative or family friend. If children talk about grandparents who have died, let them share what they are comfortable sharing.

■ Ask children to put their hand up if they have a grandparent who . . . has false teeth . . . wears fluffy slippers . . . has a beard . . . likes eating tomato soup.

TIP

This is a deliberately 'light' activity.

■ Share some of the things children have done with their grandparents.

■ Say,

You have memories of your grandparents, other people and pets. After they have died, these become really important. No one can ever take memories away. They will always be there to treasure or just think about.

■ Read the next part of the story.

When they return home, Anji and Peter take some biscuits to the beach. Marasova is by the blue goal post but he is gaspingly struggling to breathe. Anji thinks emergency fast.

'Peter, I need a towel,' she says.

And Peter knows that his sister is in charge, and he is happy with that. So he races across to Ed's shed and finds what she wants. On his way back, seagulls screech and flap their wings in front of him.

'Get lost!' he shouts at them. And for once they do as he tells them and settle their big fat bodies in a line on the cliff steps to watch as Anji wraps the towel round the turtle's shell and tucks the frayed edges inside the folds.

'Marasova, I'll look after you,' she whispers. Peter wants to whisper something to Marasova too, but he knows Anji will snap at him if he does. So he stays behind her.

'We need to take him home,' she says.

'Mum said Marasova must always stay on the beach.'

'No. This is different. Marasova is ill and needs to be where we can help him.'

Peter trails behind Anji carrying the bag with the biscuits. There are only three left by the time they reach the top of the steps. Peter hopes the two he has eaten will stop his tummy churning, but they don't.

Mum says they did the right thing and makes a special place for Marasova in the garage. He stays there for seven whole days. A lot happens that week.

MONDAY: Dad buys tickets so he and Peter can watch Chelsea next month. They are playing Wigan and Anji decides that from now on she will support Wigan.

Mr Hawkins does not give 5H any homework because it is his birthday.

TUESDAY: Peter is chosen to play in the school football team for the first time ever – on Thursday.

In the evening, while Mum is at work, Dad makes a burningly spicy curry and wiggles his nostrils as he eats it. Peter and Anji get the giggles and their faces go bright red.

WEDNESDAY: Peter has saved enough pocket money to buy a new kite from the sports shop.

THURSDAY: Holcolme Juniors Under 9 Football Team lose to Jasper Primary School. Five – nil!

Mr Hawkins tells them that playing fairly is more important than winning. Dougie says Mr Hawkins says that after every match.

FRIDAY: Anji gets a certificate in good work assembly.

SATURDAY: It is windy so the children visit the beach to fly Peter's new kite and it is brilliant!

'I wish Marasova could be here to see this,' Peter says to Anji.

SUNDAY: Marasova whispers, 'I feel better today.'

And that is the best thing that happens all week.

■ On whiteboards or paper, ask children to draw someone who is ill. Share what they draw with a partner.

TIP

Lots of these are likely to be pictures of people vomiting.

Enjoy these then highlight one or two that are about long-term illness.

■ Ask,

What might it be like to have someone at home who is unwell for a very long time?

■ Say,

Sometimes when people are very ill they can be a bit grumpy because they are feeling so unwell. That can be hard for those around them.

■ Read the next part of the story.

Peter sometimes has ideas; the sort Anji wishes she could have.

One day he says to her,

'Why don't we go to the beach when Marasova is asleep, and paint his shell bright yellow?'

Why hadn't they thought of doing that before?

'We'll have to go when it is dark,' Anji says.

Peter nods. That is partly why he thinks it is such a good idea; he knows Anji is really, really scared of the dark.

And he isn't.

So Anji finds some yellow paint and when Mum and Dad are watching television and think their children are asleep in bed, Anji and Peter sneak downstairs and out of the back door. Anji carries the bag Nina gave her for her birthday. Dad's expensive torch is in the other hand.

■ What are Peter and Anji wearing?

TIP

Elaborate on pyjamas having interesting motifs and patterns such as frogs and a Chelsea logo. Such details help children engage more with the story.

The garden is creepily still. Even the gulls are silent. Peter knows there are no pirates or wild animals around, but still decides to stay close to his sister, just in case she needs him and because she has the torch. As they reach the gate at the top of the cliff steps, Anji suddenly grabs Peter's left hand.

'Oi, you don't have to hold my hand,' he whispers and is pleased because his voice is steady and calm.

'I thought you might fall over the cliff,' she says.

'You didn't. You were scared,' Peter whispers. 'You're a pink chicken.'

'I'm not!' she says, letting go of his hand.

'Chicken,' he whispers, though he does agree that the wooden steps do seem very steep in the eerily silver moonlight.

■ Why are Anji and Peter painting Marasova?

TIP

Steer answers to cover that Anji and Peter are trying to help Marasova cheer up after his illness.

They find Marasova near Ed's shed. He looks like a huge pebble. Anji passes the torch to Peter.

'Do not drop it,' she mouths as he wraps his fingers round the cold metal casing, 'and don't shine it on Marasova in case it wakes him up.'

He knew that already.

Anji carefully opens her bag. Inside are two paintbrushes and a tube of yellow paint.

'We need some water,' she whispers. So they both stand up to tiptoe across to the shed to find a bucket.

'Is the sea colder at night?' Peter whispers, but Anji does not answer.

Peter turns round to see where she is but she has disappeared.

At least he has the torch and Anji must be behind the shed.

So he walks right round it.

But she is not there.

'Anji!' he whispers.

Silence.

'Anji,' he whispers again only this time his voice is tremblingly scared.

'Where are you?'

Silence.

'Anji,' he whispers again.

His whisper is rewarded by a giggle and Anji jumps out from the side of the shed.

'Who's the chicken now?' she whispers.

'I looked behind the shed,' he whispers back.

'And shone the torch in front of you so I knew when you were coming and ran ahead. Blue chicken!'

'I'm not!' he hisses and he knows his voice is still trembling, just a little bit.

And Anji, just for a brief moment wonders whether she shouldn't have hidden. And then she suddenly feels guilty about borrowing Dad's very expensive torch without asking. It was a present from Grandad before he died. And then she thinks about Mum and Dad not knowing where they are and what will happen if they look in their bedrooms and find empty beds. Anji is meant to be more sensible than Peter because she is ten and he is only eight. She wishes she had left a note on her pillow saying where they were.

'Come on!' she says. 'Let's be quick.'

'We must be extra sensible,' she adds and Peter nods and knows, unlike her, that he is already being so.

■ Anji feels guilty? Why?

In pairs, ask children to come up with a definition of guilt, including examples.

■ Say,

> Guilt is feeling bad because you think you have made something nasty happen.

TIP

Many children feel guilty when someone is ill and blame themselves. So it is good to remind children to find something they have done that is positive, such as making a card or visiting them or keeping quiet. This might help them feel less guilty.

■ Ask,

> How might guilt make you feel inside?

■ Ask,

> Peter and Anji had a great week when Marasova was ill. Do you think they might have felt guilty about it afterwards? Why? Why not?

■ Divide a piece of paper or a whiteboard into two columns and write headings of 'did feel guilty' and 'did not feel guilty' at the top of them. Ask children to jot down reasons why Anji and Peter might have felt guilty or not guilty. After a couple of minutes, share their answers.

■ Highlight that even when children feel guilty, there is always a reason *not* to feel guilty as well.

■ Remind children of turtle dictionary words frillda (grey), grilopsi (yellow), mumin (stupid), spluff (gull) and umpo (gull poo) then read the next section of the story.

Next morning, Peter and Anji race down to the beach. Marasova is hiding behind Ed's shed.

'What's wrong?' Anji asks. 'Don't you like your shell?'

'I love it,' he whispers. 'But the mumin spluffs keep dumping umpo on me.'

'They what?' Anji explodes.

'They dive bomb me with umpo.'

'Mumin spluffs!' Peter shouts, 'I'll kill the lot of them!'

'How?' Anji asks in her big sister voice.

'Sometimes,' Marasova says quietly, 'things happen that you cannot do anything about. Today, the spluffs have a new game called Dumping Umpo. I cannot change that. You'd better make me frillda again.' Then he adds, 'but thank you for trying. It was such a lovely idea.'

'Mum cleans her paintbrushes with white spirit,' Anji says sadly. 'I'll go and fetch some.'

'How much umpo can a spluff make in one day?' Peter asks as Anji starts walking back towards the cliff steps. He has found his football and is dribbling it in a most annoying way, as if he is dancing with it.

'Stop asking ridiculously stupid questions,' she snaps.

There is a pause then Peter suddenly kicks the ball and it slams into Anji's left shoulder. He aimed it at her deliberately and she wants to thump him but knows he'll tell Mum – and probably cry pathetic little tears as well. So she takes a deep breath and walks away.

Two days later they are watching television when Peter says,

'I've just had another idea.' And it is another good one, which secretly annoys Anji because she wants to have good ideas like her squirty little brother does.

'We know how to make you grilopsi *and* beat the mumin spluffs,' the children tell Marasova next time they go down to the beach.

'It was my idea,' Peter says.

'And I found the polish,' Anji adds.

'The grilopsi polish,' Marasova chuckles as they show him the tin.

TIP

Make sure children know this is furniture polish and not shoe polish.

So the children paint Marasova bright yellow, wait for the paint to dry then plaster his shell with polish. He waddles on to the open sand, pulls his head and legs in to his shell and waits for the spluffs to squawkily line up and glide towards him.

But this time the umpo gracefully slides off his shell. The children cheer and Peter writes MUMIN SPLUFFS ARE LOSERS in the sand and wiggles his bottom at them.

'This is the day we beat the spluffs,' Anji shouts.

Then Peter says, 'How big is a gull's brain?'

'About an eighth the size of a ping pong ball,' Anji says.

'Can they read?'

'No.'

'So they won't know what I have written in the sand.'

'No.'

'I don't care. They are still losers!'

A few weeks later, glisteningly white snowflakes cover everything. Anji and Peter take yumgo and pilchards down to Marasova and make sure he is all right.

'Everyone builds snowmen,' Anji says, 'but we are going to make a snow turtle with pebbles for eyes and seaweed for legs.'

'And I will watch you,' Marasova says, 'from the safety of Ed's shed.'

When the snow turtle is finished, Peter and Anji lie down in the snow, flap their arms up and down to make angel wings then throw snowballs at each other. Their fingers feel like they will drop off because they are so freezingly cold but Anji and Peter don't care because they are having such a brilliantly wicked time.

'I want to remember this day forever and ever and ever,' Peter says, 'but I do wish snow was warm.'

'Warm and pink would be even better,' Anji says.

'Pink snow would be stupid,' Peter says.

Later, as they climb back up the steps, Peter says,

'When it gets warm and the snow turtle melts, does it mean he's died?'

Anji stares at her brother's wellies two steps in front of her. Very slowly, she says,

'Peter, that snow turtle is not real. He is not alive.' And she's hoping he will give up and think of something else.

But he doesn't.

Instead he says, 'If he is not real, does that mean he is dead?'

'Peter, the snow turtle cannot die. He is made out of snow. He is not alive. Move your left wellie if you understand?'

But Peter does not move anything.

'How do I know I'm not going to melt when we go home and I get warm again?' he suddenly says.

'You will completely melt into nothing if you keep asking stupid questions,' she says.

But they are not stupid to Peter.

'So will I melt?' he asks again.

''Course you won't,' she says.

■ Ask,

> What do you think you will remember about being a child when you are older? Share ideas with the class.

■ Say,

> We have thought about memories and how they can become even more important after someone has died. We have thought about what it's like when someone is seriously ill; it can be really tough for everyone but it's okay to find it tough. We've also thought about guilt because when Marasova was ill, Anji and Peter might have forgotten about the helpful things they did for him. And there is one more thing to remember. Nothing anyone says, and nothing anyone thinks, can cause someone to die.

■ Let children draw as they begin to process what has been thought about.

4 CARING FOR EACH OTHER WHEN SOMEONE DIES

Children think about how a community might support people who are very ill and how we might feel after someone we know dies.

Preparation

It is important to be aware of any children who are bereaved so that you are prepared to respond appropriately to any comments they may make or reactions they may have.

Have paper ready to make a card for Anji and Peter.

■ Revisit the ground rules.

1 You don't have to share something if you feel it is too private.
2 Listen carefully to each other.

TIP

Recapping the third rule is especially important today.

3 After someone dies, some people feel very sad and other people might not feel anything at all. We're all different and it is okay not to feel the same as other people do.

Today we are thinking about how people might support each other when someone is hurting.

TIP

In order to keep this lesson objective, when working with the whole class, keep the focus on the story rather than your personal experiences.

■ On whiteboards or paper, ask children to write a list of feelings talked about so far in the story.

■ Quickly make a list on the board of their collective ideas, recapping events that led to the feelings.

■ Read the next part of the story.

Roads are still icy and school is still closed. So Mum decides Anji will spend the next day tidying her room. Completely – every cupboard, every box, every shelf. How boring is that!

The good thing is that Mum helps and together they collect toys and books and clothes to take to the charity shop when the weather improves. Dad works on his laptop in the back room and Peter plays on his PlayStation until he becomes hungry and raids the chocolate biscuit tin in the kitchen.

As he sneaks out of the kitchen for the second time he sees Anji's old doll's house by the front door.

'Don't take the doll's house to the charity shop,' he shouts. 'Marasova could live in it. It's even got a yellow front door.'

So a few days later, when the snow has melted and Anji's room is untidy again, they carry the doll's house to the beach and put it next to Ed's shed.

'Thank you!' Marasova chuckles. 'It's even got a balcony for you to leave food on.'

But as soon as the children leave the beach, what should skim across the sand but . . . the spluffs. They have a new game called Fly-As-Close-As-You-Can-But-Don't-Hit-the-House.

'I knew they'd be back sometime,' Marasova sighs. 'And I know what is going to happen. One of them will . . .'

And one of them does. The baby spluff flies smashingly straight into the roof, cartwheels over the top and dribbles across the sand.

When Anji and Peter next come down to the beach, Marasova's house is full of a grumbly ugly gull.

'What are you doing?' Anji says. 'That house is for you, not a spluff.'

'The spluff is injured,' Marasova says, 'so I am looking after her until she is mended. She's called Dribble.'

'Dribble! You've given that spluff a name?'

'I have to call her something.'

And while her wing mends, Marasova becomes Dribble's friend. In fact, he becomes friends with all the spluffs and gives them all names. They won't be nasty to him again and even agree to fly out to sea if they are having an argument.

'I still want to be covered in polish though,' Marasova tells the children, 'because I like the shine it puts on my yellow shell, and I like the smell.'

The children laugh. They love this beach. One day they might even learn to love the spluffs as well. Only they're not called spluffs anymore. They're called Dribble, Sybil, Fizzle, Wiggle and Chelsea.

Chelsea!

What a ridiculous name for a seagull!

■ Say,

> Marasova was ill. Anji and Peter tried to cheer him up by painting his shell.
>
> Dribble's wing is mending but can you think about what it is like for someone who is not just a bit ill, but very, very ill for a long time and is not getting better?

■ Ask,

> What do people who are very ill do and what don't they do?
>
> What is the very worst thing that can happen to an ill person?
> The answer 'dying' is not allowed.

> **TIP**
>
> Encourage the answers to the first question to be light. For example, they don't go sand dancing or run the marathon. By having some lighter moments, children feel they are more in control of the lesson content. They do stay in bed, don't want to eat and even watching the telly is too much.

- Draw a picture in the middle of a whiteboard or piece of paper of someone ill in bed. Then draw and label all the people who might be able to help that person. Ask children to draw a box round the person who can help an ill person the most and think about why they have chosen that person.

- Share ideas with the class.

> **TIP**
>
> Make sure 'friends' are mentioned.

- When children say doctors and nurses, say,

  Most of the time, doctors and nurses do make people better but sometimes people are too ill for the medicines to work.

- Read the next part of the story.

Anji has a new pair of wellies. They are pink and she wants to show Marasova. Peter is clutching the certificate Mr Hawkins gave him in assembly for scoring a goal in last week's football match.

Nothing stirs as Peter opens the front panel of Marasova's house, so he lays his certificate on the table in Ed's shed. Anji goes to the water's edge to check that her wellies really are waterproof. They are, but as she stands in the shallow water she feels uneasy about Marasova. He always wakes up when they visit him, even if he goes back to sleep again. So she plods back up the beach and pulls the front panel of Marasova's house wide open. Gently, she slides her hand under his shell to lift him out.

TIP

Keep reading as normal, though if you normally read with lots of emotion and expression, reduce the emotion.

For a split second, everything freezes, as if she is inside a bubble. Slowly, she realises what has happened. Half of her still wonders whether Marasova will suddenly move and chuckle, but . . .

'I want to show Marasova my back heel,' Peter says behind her. She can hear his trainers scuffing against the sand and the football bouncing up and down.

And all Anji can say is,

'Peter, Marasova's not moving.'

'He will in a minute,' Peter says.

He wants her to say that Marasova is all right.

But she can't.

'Peter,' she whispers, standing up, 'he's dead.'

Tears are rolling down her cheeks.

'He can't be,' Peter says. 'We left him some sardines yesterday.'

'He hasn't touched them,' Anji whispers.

The football rolls down the beach as Anji puts her arms round her little brother. They cling to each other and it is okay to cry. There's an aching in their throats. They love Marasova. He is their friend. He is part of their family. Only now he is gone. And it hurts. All over, like it will never stop.

They have memories of him: sitting on top of sandcastles when they fought the tide, in the dinghy, his chuckle, that awful time when they thought the current had swept him out to sea, him watching them make snow turtles, carrying him up the steps when he was ill, buying polish and yumgo with their pocket money, when Fizzle stole his birthday cake – though that was ages ago, when he first came from the Big Sea. He'd helped Peter get in the school football team. He'd helped Anji learn her spellings.

And now he was gone. He would never chuckle or talk to them again. Ever.

Peter suddenly pulls away and kneels down next to Marasova's house.

'What are you doing?' Anji whispers.

'Look,' he says and holds up two pebbles. One is blue and the other is pink. 'It's like . . . it's like Marasova's left us a present.'

Anji stares at the pebbles. She imagines she can hear Marasova talking to her now. But all Anji can really hear are the gulls high in the sky and the waves running over the sand.

'We must tell Mum and Dad,' she whispers. 'And . . . and I want to tell Marasova about my pink wellies. Even though he is dead, I can still write a letter to him.'

'If you put your letter in a big envelope,' Peter whispers, 'can I put my football certificate in it as well?'

Anji nods and hugs her little brother once more. They are in this together as they walk back towards the cliff steps. And as they do, their footprints leave a trail in the sand.

TIP

This next activity helps children start processing what the story is about. Go straight on to it.

■ Say,

> Over the last few weeks, the feelings we have thought about, many of which are on the board, are feelings Anji and Peter might feel after Marasova has died.

> Remember the ground rules each week? We are all different and Anji and Peter might feel all of the feelings or just some of them.

■ Ask children to think of four or five feelings Anji and Peter might be feeling right now when they have just found out that Marasova is dead. There are no right or wrong answers.

■ Stand up and find a friend to share your chosen feelings with.

TIP

Moving round will relieve tension. If some children are crying, reassure them that this is okay because the story is sad. Then encourage them to join in the activity.

■ Ask,

> What do you think someone who did not know Marasova might feel about him dying?

33

TIP

Refer back to the ground rules if need be; everyone reacts differently.

■ In pairs, ask children to write down one or two things they might do to help if someone who is important to one of their friends died. Then read out some of the list below. If the children have similar things, they can tick them off.

TIP

Some of these are deliberately light-hearted to relieve tension through laughter. Read through them quickly.

1 Be a good friend (explore what this means and refer back to the ground rules of listening and not having to share things that are too private).

2 Take them to the fish and chip shop.

3 Let them sit next to you and not say anything.

4 Listen carefully to what they are saying.

5 Ignore them (because you feel awkward and embarrassed).

6 If you don't feel sad, don't suddenly pretend you are.

7 Go to a football match with them.

8 Talk to them about the person who has died.

9 Hang out with them like you usually do.

10 Do something with them and include a few other people as well.

TIP

Emphasise that pretending is not helpful. Someone who is bereaved needs people to be honest.

11 Cry with them.

12 If you are not the person's best friend, try not to suddenly pretend you are.

13 Treat the person normally but remember they might be feeling a bit wobbly at times.

14 Play a game but don't deliberately let them win.

15 Try not to be fed up with them if they are angry and upset.

16 Keep being there for them but make sure you have other friends to be with as well.

17 Maybe go to the funeral with them if that feels like the right thing to do.

■ Say,

> If it is someone's birthday we send cards to let them know we are thinking about them. We do the same if someone dies. We're going to design a card to send to Peter and Anji to let them know that we are thinking about them because a friend of theirs (Marasova) has died.

■ Hand out paper for children to make a card. This is a time to chat to children as they draw.

TIP

If asked about funerals, explain that it is a special ceremony to say 'good-bye' to someone who has died. People do different things, depending on what they believe, or whether they have a religious faith.

■ Say,

> Today we've thought about what we and other people might do to help someone who is very, very ill. Sadly, not everyone who is ill gets better because sometimes they are too unwell for medicines to work. We've thought about how we might feel after someone we know dies and how we might help a friend if someone important to them has died.

35

TIP

The activity may have stirred up difficult feelings in some children so it is essential to reassure all the class and remind those who feel they need it where to go for support.

All life has a beginning and an ending; it is part of the life cycle. Most people die when they are old but sadly some die when they are young. It is okay to talk about people who have died, or who are dying. Remember, in school there are people who will listen to you if there is anything you want to talk about, no matter what it is.

■ On paper or whiteboards, let children draw anything they want to.

For children aged 7–9

Children think about special places, special people, feelings and wishes they make. Throughout, the term 'children' refers to those listening to and interacting with the story. The children in the story text are referred to as Peter and Anji.

Preparation

Download pictures in this order: a) unpopulated beach, b) steps leading down a cliff face to a beach, c) blue and yellow blow-up dinghy, d) a turtle.

Further pictures will be added each session.

■ Explain that this story is about feelings, including feelings we might have after someone has died. To help children feel safe, certain ground rules need to be talked about . . .

   1   You don't have to share something if you feel it is too private.
   2   Listen carefully to each other.
   3   After someone dies, some people feel very sad and other people might not feel anything at all. We're all different and it is okay not to feel the same as other people do.

TIP

Phrases and concepts that need careful wording or explanation are written so they can be used directly from the script. These are indicated by the word 'Say' or 'Ask' written on a line with the question or comment on the line below.

■ Look at a picture of an empty beach on the whiteboard. Ask children to think of one thing that could be added to the picture. Use this to introduce beach vocabulary. Then look at pictures of a cliff with steps and a blue and yellow dinghy.

■ Read the first part of the story.

Peter is always asking questions. Today, he and Anji are on their way to the beach at the bottom of their garden. Peter says,
'Who built these steps?' and Anji says,
'Little green aliens.'
'No they didn't,' Peter says.
'They did.'
'Didn't,' Peter shouts.
'Did. Stupid,' Anji yells.
Then Mum, who is in front of them says,
'Oy, you two, stop arguing.'
Mum is helping Dad carry a huge cardboard box. Inside the box are two oars, a foot pump and a yellow and blue blow-up dinghy. It is a present from Granny.

■ Ask children to choose a character to follow in the story – Mum, Dad, Anji or Peter – and think about what feelings their character has.

When they reach the sand, Dad uses the foot pump to inflate the dinghy. Then he smiles at Mum,
'You take the boat out first, with Anji,' he says. 'Peter and I have something special we want to do.'
'Like what?' Mum asks, but Dad just smiles and says nothing.
'What are you up to?' she asks.
'You'll find out,' he says and smiles at her again.

■ What feelings are the four characters feeling now? Make a vertical list of feelings children suggest on the left-hand side of the board.

Dad and Peter help Anji and Mum in to the boat and push them out on the water. Gulls fly above them as Mum helps Anji pull on the oars so the front of the boat cuts through the water. Having a beach as part of your garden is brilliant. Having a little boat as well is the best thing ever.

And then Mum says,

'Look what those two are doing!'

Anji looks back towards the beach.

Her mouth drops open.

She cannot believe what she can see.

■ Ask children what they think Dad and Peter are doing back on the beach.

Dad and Peter are painting a goal post on the cliff face, in bright blue paint. 'We've got to go back and stop them!' Mum shouts. 'They cannot do that.' But they can, and they have.

■ How are the characters feeling now?

■ Add further words to the list on the board.

When Anji and Mum get back to the beach Dad says,

'Don't worry. The paint will wear off in a few months.' And then Mum suddenly starts laughing because the blue goal post lines are very wiggly and Dad has blue paint on his nose and on his chin and on his shorts and on his fingers. So Anji starts laughing too. Not in a nasty way, but because she knows that the beach and her family, even her little brother, are so very, very special.

■ What other feelings could be added to the list?

■ Ask children to tell their partner where their favourite place is and who their favourite people are.

When they are in their favourite place or with their favourite people, do they have any feelings that are in the list on the board?

Share this with a partner.

- While children are doing this, write these turtle dictionary words on the right-hand side of the board.

    cranthi – hello
    frillda – grey
    spluff – seagull
    mumin – stupid
    grilopsi – yellow
    yumgo – chocolate cake

- Look at a picture of a turtle so children know what one is.

- Ask children why they think the words have been written on the right-hand side of the board. They will find out as the next part of the story is read.

For years the children have the beach all to themselves; until Marasova arrives one day after a storm.

'Cranthi,' he says in a croaky voice, 'pleased to meet you.'

Peter and Anji stare at him and the weird thing is that they both understand what he says, even though he speaks in his own language.

'That turtle just said "hello, pleased to meet you",' Peter whispers.

'I know,' Anji says.

'Where have you come from?' Peter asks him.

'The Big Sea,' Marasova says. 'I like this beach though. It's a lovely place for a turtle to live.'

'He must have a birthday,' Mum says and as October 1st is the next time the children visit the beach, they decide that October 1st will be his birthday. They have a fancy dress birthday party for him.

- Ask children what dressing up clothes they would wear if they were going to Marasova's party.

'Marasova, how old do you want to be?' Peter asks.

'Eight,' he says. 'Then I am one year older than you and one year younger than your sister.'

'Make a wish,' Peter says as Marasova blows out the candles on his birthday yumgo.

'I am bored being frillda, so I wish . . . that my shell was grilopsi.' Then Marasova laughs. 'My shell will never change,' he says, 'because it can't.'

'You're not supposed to tell anyone what you wish!' Anji says.

'I didn't know that,' Marasova says. 'Can a wish really change something?'

Then he thanks the children for his birthday yumgo. He has never had one before.

Neither has the big fat spluff who suddenly swoops down, sticks its beak into the yellow sugar icing and takes off again with the yumgo hanging from its beak.

'Oy!' Peter shouts as the cake disappears, 'give that back!'

But all the spluff does is drop a sticky splat of poo right in front of Peter's left foot.

'Stupid seagull,' Peter shouts at it, 'you nearly hit me.'

On the way home, as they climb back up the steps, Peter says to Anji,

'Why do you keep birthday wishes secret?'

And Anji says,

'Because you might wish for something that is silly.'

Peter thinks about this, then he says,

'Marasova wishing he was bright yellow was a bit silly, wasn't it?'

■ Ask children what, in the story, could and could not happen in real life.

> **TIP**
>
> Marasova does NOT morph into other things or do magic tricks. He talks and knows about Anji and Peter's life but is still semi-constrained by physical things a turtle can do. He also has feelings.

■ Ask them to divide a whiteboard or piece of paper into four and label the boxes A, B, C, and D. In the sections write down and draw . . .

A A wish you made when you wished you had done something differently, e.g.,

– *I wish I had remembered to tell my brother to bring his football with him*

– *If only I had worn my coat*

– *I wish I hadn't told that lie*

B An impossible/ridiculous wish that could never come true, e.g.,

– *I wish I was a (named) pop star/footballer*

– *I wish my birthday was in June*

C A wish you once made that came true, e.g.,

- *I wish Arsenal would score a goal*
- *I wish my friend could come round and play*

D A wish where, if you did something, you could make the wish come true, e.g.,

- *I wish I could learn my tables*
- *I'd love to see that film*

If children cannot think of any wishes, let them use one of the examples given above.

TIP

Keep tasks short and sharp. Allow two to three minutes for drawing tasks – enough to record thoughts but not resemble an art lesson.

■ Ask children to tell their partner about feelings that would have accompanied each wish they thought of. Remind them they don't have to share anything they don't want to.

■ In summary, say,

Today we have thought about feelings and wishes. Some feelings might have been happy ones, some sad. These are feelings everyone has and we are learning about them now; even when you get older you will still be learning about them.

Wishes are important too; sometimes they can come true and sometimes they can't.

■ Let children draw anything they like from the story so far. This is to give them time to start processing what has been thought about during the lesson.

2 FOOTBALL TEAMS, BUILDING SANDCASTLES AND LOSING MARASOVA

Children think about their response to things they cannot control. One possible response is anger. They then think how they might feel when someone important to them has gone.

Preparation

Download and add pictures of building sandcastles and fighting the tide to previous pictures.

■ On whiteboards or paper, ask children to draw one thing they remember from the story last time. Share their pictures with the class to recap what happened in the story.

■ Revisit the ground rules.

   1   You don't have to share something if you feel it is too private.
   2   Listen carefully to each other.
   3   After someone dies, some people feel very sad and other people might not feel anything at all. We're all different and it is okay not to feel the same as other people do.

■ Say,

   Today we are thinking about when things happen that we cannot control and how that might make us feel. We're also going to think about how we might feel if someone or something that is important to us goes missing.

■ Look at pictures of children building sandcastles and fighting the tide. Make sure children understand what these are.

■ Read the next part of the story.

'I wish I was in the Year 3 football team,' Peter says.

'You'll just have to practise kicking the ball in to the wiggly blue goal on the cliff face,' Marasova says. 'If you want, I'll help you get better; but not today because I want to build a sandcastle and try and stop the tide knocking it down.'

The sandcastle they build is enormous and when it is finished, Anji and Peter lift Marasova on top of it.

'I'm the king of the castle,' he chuckles and waggles his legs.

He stays there until the tide comes in and makes the sand collapse. When it does, Marasova slides into the water and swims out to sea leaving the children to jump on the mound that is left. They want to flatten it before the waves do. As they jump, Peter accidentally bumps into Anji,

'Oy!' she shouts at him. 'What did you do that for?'

Then she turns on him, pushing Peter out of the way.

'You're little and you're weak and . . .'

Peter throws himself at her legs. He hates it when she is nasty to him and makes him feel small. They both fall over into the sea.

'I'm not little,' he shouts.

'Oh yes you are,' she says and pushes him back into the water.

'I'm not weak either,' he yells.

'Oh yes you are. And you're pathetic and you're probably going to start crying now.'

And Peter hurts inside because his best friend, Ahmed, is playing in the Year 3 football team next week, and Peter isn't. Suddenly he hates everybody, especially Anji, and he turns away so she cannot see the tears in his eyes.

And high above, seagulls squawk and he thinks they are laughing at him because he is so small and useless and cannot do anything.

■ At the top of the board, draw a horizontal line and write 'happy' on the left-hand side of it and 'angry' on the right-hand side. Ask children to suggest a few words related to feelings – e.g., excited, worried – and where each should be written on the line.

TIP

Use this as an opportunity to reinforce that people see things differently. Invite children to the board to write a feeling where they think it should go on the line.

■ Make sure there are some angry words to show different strengths of emotions, such as . . . *irritating, withdrawn, fuming, moody, cross, livid, quietly exploding, incandescent with rage, snappy, annoyed, crabby, crotchety, cantankerous, fractious, incensed, seething, furious, tetchy, grouchy, short-tempered, bad-tempered, peeved, miserable.*

- Ask children to think of things they cannot control and write them down on their whiteboards; e.g., *the weather, the date of their birthday, death, the time of their favourite TV programme.*

  On the board, underneath the angry/happy line, write down a few things the children cannot control. (Don't use up too much space as there is something else to be written down as well.)

- Not being in control made Peter angry. How did it make him behave?

- On whiteboards or paper, ask children to draw what they think of when they hear the word . . . 'anger'. Draw for about two minutes, then share what children have drawn.

TIP

Encourage children to draw in silence.

- Remind children they do not have to share anything if they don't want to.

- Ask,

  Have you ever taken your anger out on anyone else? What happened? Share answers with a partner.

- Ask,

  How might you help yourself when you are feeling angry? Take children's answers and make a list on the board, underneath the happy/angry line.

- Then read the next part of the story.

Marasova loves lying on the front of the dinghy. Behind him, Peter and Anji sit side by side in their life jackets, one oar each, rowing towards the orange markers which are as far as they are allowed to row. It is dangerous if they go past them; they might be swept out into the Big Sea.

Peter is really pleased because he is rowing the boat as fast as Anji is. A few months ago he could not do this. He turns round to tell Marasova.

But Marasova is not there.

'Where is he?' Peter asks.

'He'll have dropped in the sea and gone for a swim,' Anji says. But Peter shakes his head.

'Marasova always pops up to let us know where he is,' Peter says. 'Has he got trapped underneath the boat?'

'He'll be all right,' Anji says. 'He can swim underwater.'

But Peter says,

'Where is he then?'

They both stare into the deep swirling sea.

'Has he gone out past the orange markers?' Peter says.

'How should I know?' Anji says.

'Should we row out and have a look?' Peter says.

'No,' Anji says straight away. 'Mum and Dad have said we must never ever go past the orange markers.'

'But he might be out there.'

'We are not going,' Anji says. 'It is not safe out there.'

'How strong are Marasova's legs?' Peter asks.

'He'll be all right,' Anji says quickly and is pleased her voice doesn't show how worried she is. Peter is right. Marasova does always let them know where he is. Why hasn't he done that today?

'Can turtles hold their breath for a long time?' Peter asks.

'Of course they can.'

Then he says,

'If Marasova is dragged out to the Big Sea, how can Mum and Dad find him again?'

And they both know what the answer to that question is.

Anji says,

'Let's row back to the beach.'

It is like something awful has happened but neither of them wants to talk about it.

'Marasova's gone, hasn't he?' Peter whispers. 'He's gone back to the Big Sea. I don't want him to do that. I love him being on our beach. Did he go back because we argued with each other?'

All Anji says is,

'I don't know.'

The gulls are squawking as the children drag the dinghy on to the beach.

'We'd better tell Mum and Dad,' Anji says.

'Why did Marasova leave?' Peter asks in a small voice.

'I just don't know,' Anji says.

'What don't you know?' a voice says behind them.

Both children spin round.

A turtle is looking up at them with a big grin on his wrinkled face.

'I've had a great swim,' he says.

'But we've been so worried,' Anji says, but suddenly the sun is shining and everyone is smiling and Peter's ribcage stops hurting.

- Ask,

    How might Peter and Anji have felt when they realised Marasova was no longer in the dinghy with them?

- Ask children to share with a partner when they have felt the same.

- Ask children to draw something they have lost and how they felt about it.

> **TIP**
>
> If children cannot think of anything, they can draw Peter and Anji realising Marasova was not in the boat.

- In summary, say,

    Today we have thought about when things happen and we cannot always control them. It might make us feel angry. It could also make us feel scared and helpless, especially if something or someone who is really important goes missing.

- Let children draw anything from the story to give them space to start processing what has been talked about.

3 SEVEN DAYS AND THEN MARASOVA IS PAINTED

Children think about grandparents, when someone is ill, what might make us feel guilty and the importance of memories.

Preparation

Download pictures of home-made biscuits and a granny with false teeth and add to previous pictures.

■ Revisit the ground rules.

1 You don't have to share something if you feel it is too private.
2 Listen carefully to each other.
3 After someone dies, some people feel very sad and other people might not feel anything at all. We're all different and it is okay not to feel the same as other people do.

■ Recap the story by looking at pictures from the previous two sessions and then at the home-made biscuits and false teeth.

■ Today we are thinking about remembering our grandparents, what happens when someone is ill and what might make us feel guilty.

Anji and Peter visit Granny. They decorate pebbles and shells from the beach before they go.

The pink shells are Anji's, the yellow ones are Marasova's and Peter's are blue because he supports Chelsea.

Granny supports Chelsea too.

So does Dad.

Anji and Mum do not.

Granny helps them make biscuits, wears false teeth and talks to Grandad's picture on top of the television. Grandad died two years ago.

'I still miss him,' Granny tells Anji. 'Do you remember the noise his motorbike made when he drove out of the garage?' She does. It was very loud.

Anji and Peter miss Grandad too. He used to play football and cards with them and sent emails with funny pictures on that made them laugh.

■ On whiteboards or paper, ask children to write about or draw a picture of something they have done with their grandparents.

TIP

If children have never known their grandparents, let them draw pictures of things they have done with another relative or family friend. If children talk about grandparents who have died, let them share what they are comfortable sharing.

- Ask children to put their hand up if they have a grandparent who has false teeth . . . wears fluffy slippers . . . has a beard . . . likes eating tomato soup.

  Then share some of the things children have done with their grandparents.

TIP

This is deliberately a 'light' activity.

- Say,

  You have memories of your grandparents, other people and pets. After they have died, these will become really important. No one can ever take memories away. They will always be there to treasure or just think about.

- Read the next part of the story.

On Sunday, when Anji and Peter arrive home, they go to the beach. It is a good thing they do because something is wrong with Marasova and he is gasping for breath.

Anji says, 'Peter, Marasova's ill. Go to the shed and fetch a towel.'

And Peter does as she says because something is very wrong and Anji is in charge and making decisions about what to do.

Very gently, Anji wraps the towel round the turtle's shell.

'I'll look after you, my little friend' she whispers. Peter wants to whisper something to Marasova as well, but knows Anji will snap at him if he does. So he stays where he is, watching.

'We need to take Marasova home,' Anji suddenly says.

'But Mum says he must always stay on the beach.'

'No,' Anji says, 'he needs to be where we can help him.' And she carefully picks up the turtle and carries him across the sand and up the steps.

When they tell Mum, she says they have done the right thing bringing him home and makes a special place for him in the garage. He stays there for seven whole days and sleeps most of the time.

A lot happens that week.

MONDAY: Dad buys tickets so he and Peter can watch Chelsea next month.

TUESDAY: Peter is chosen to play in the school football team for the first time ever. The match is on Thursday. He is so excited, he tells Anji at playtime.

WEDNESDAY: Peter has saved his pocket money for eight weeks so now has enough money to buy a new kite.

THURSDAY: Holcolme Juniors Under 8 Football Team lose their football match 5–0. Five – nil!

FRIDAY: Anji is given a good work certificate in assembly for writing a story about a cat with a curly tail.

SATURDAY: It is windy so the children visit the beach to fly Peter's new kite and it is brilliant!

'I wish Marasova could be here to see this,' Peter says to Anji.

SUNDAY: Marasova whispers,

'I feel better today.'

And that is the best thing that happens all week.

■ On whiteboards or paper, ask children to draw someone who is ill.

Share what they have drawn.

TIP

Lots of these are likely to be pictures of people vomiting. Enjoy these then highlight one or two that are about long-term illness.

■ Ask,

What might it be like to have someone at home who is unwell for a very long time?

■ Say,

Sometimes when people are very ill they can be a bit grumpy because they are feeling so unwell. That can be hard for those around them.

■ Read the next part of the story.

Sometimes Peter has great ideas.

Like when he says to Anji,

'You know Marasova wants to be bright yellow. Why don't we go to the beach when he is asleep and paint his shell?'

'We'll have to go when it is dark,' Anji says.

Peter nods. That is partly why he thinks it is such a good idea.

So Anji finds some yellow paint and when Mum and Dad are watching the television and think their children are asleep in bed, Anji and Peter tiptoe downstairs and out of the back door. Anji has a bag in her left hand and Dad's expensive torch in the other.

■ What are Peter and Anji wearing?

TIP

Elaborate on pyjamas having interesting motifs and patterns such as frogs or a Chelsea logo. Such details help children engage more with the story.

The garden is silent. Even the gulls have gone to sleep. Peter stays very close to his sister – just in case she needs him. When they reach the gate at the top of the cliff steps, Anji suddenly grabs Peter's left hand and squeezes it very tight.

'Why are you holding my hand?' Peter says.

'I thought you might fall over the cliff,' she says.

'You didn't,' Peter whispers. 'You are scared. You're just a pink chicken!'

'I am not!' she says, letting go of his hand.

They find Marasova near the shed. He is asleep. Anji passes the torch to Peter.

'Do not drop it,' she whispers. He holds it very tight, making sure the light does not fall on Marasova's face in case it wakes him up.

Anji carefully opens her bag. Inside are two paintbrushes and a tube of yellow paint.

■ Why are Anji and Peter painting Marasova?

TIP

Steer the answers to cover that Anji and Peter are trying to help Marasova cheer up after his illness.

'We need some water,' she whispers and they both stand up to find a bucket in the shed. Peter goes first with the torch.

'Does the sea get colder at night?' Peter whispers when they are nearly there, but Anji does not answer. He looks round but she has disappeared.

Completely vanished.

Peter stands still. His heart is beating extra fast. He can't call out or he might wake Marasova.

It is obvious; Anji must be hiding behind the shed. At least he has Dad's torch. He shines the light on the ground and walks . . . right round the shed.

But she isn't there. Neither is anyone else. He is on his own. On the beach in the middle of the night and he shouldn't be. Anji should be there with him.

'Anji!' Peter whispers, 'where are you?' Then he adds, 'please come out if you are hiding. I don't like being on my own on the beach in the middle of the night.'

'Who's scared now?' a voice whispers and Anji jumps out from behind the shed.

'I looked there,' Peter whispers.

'And shone the torch in front of you so I knew when you were coming and moved round the shed. You're a blue chicken!'

'I'm not!' he says and swallows hard to stop himself crying.

'Come on!' Anji says. 'Let's do the painting and go back to bed.'

She is suddenly feeling guilty about borrowing Dad's torch without asking. She should not have done it. And maybe she should not have hidden from Peter and scared him so much. And then she feels even guiltier because Mum and Dad don't know where they are. Peter and Anji always have to tell them if they are going to the beach. She is meant to be more sensible than Peter because she is nearly 10 and he is only 7. She wishes she had left a note on her pillow saying where they were.

'We must be extra sensible,' she says to Peter who nods and knows he is already being so.

■ Anji feels guilty? Why?

■ Say,

> Guilt is feeling bad because you think you have made something nasty happen.

TIP

Many children feel guilty when someone is very ill and blame themselves. It is good to remind children to find something they have done that is positive, such as making a card or visiting them or keeping quiet. This might help them feel less guilty.

■ Ask,

> How might guilt make you feel inside?

■ Ask,

> Peter and Anji had a great week when Marasova was ill. Do you think they might have felt guilty about it afterwards? Why? Why not?

■ Divide a piece of paper or a whiteboard into two columns and write headings of 'did feel guilty' and 'did not feel guilty' at the top of them. Ask children to jot down reasons why Anji and Peter might have felt guilty or not guilty.

After a couple of minutes, share their answers as a class.

TIP

Highlight that even when children feel guilty, there is always a reason *not* to feel guilty as well.

■ Read the next part of the story.

Next morning, Peter and Anji race down to the beach. They want to know what Marasova thinks about his bright yellow shell.

But Marasova is hiding behind the shed.

'What's wrong?' Anji asks. 'Don't you like your shell?'

'I love it,' Marasova whispers. 'But the gulls keep dropping poo on me!'

'They what?'

'They keep dropping poo on me.'

'Stupid seagulls!' Peter shouts.

'Sometimes,' Marasova says quietly, 'something happens and you cannot do anything about it. Like this. We'll never change the gulls. You'd better make me grey again, but thank you for trying. It was such a lovely idea.'

'I know,' Peter suddenly says, 'why don't we put polish on you! It's yellow and the poo will run off it.'

What a brilliant idea!

Anji looks at her brother wishing she had thought of it.

TIP

Make sure children understand this is furniture polish, which is slippery, and not shoe polish.

Half an hour later Marasova walks onto the open sand, pulls his head and legs in to his shell and waits. It is not long before the gulls glide towards him.

But this time their poo does not stick to his shell and Peter takes his spade and writes WE BEAT YOU in the sand.

'Stupid seagulls!' he says.

'Mumin spluffs!' Marasova agrees.

A few weeks later, beautiful cold snowflakes cover everything and school is closed. The children take yumgo and sardines to the beach.

'Everyone builds snowmen,' Anji says, 'but we are going to make a snow turtle.'

'And I shall watch you from the shed,' Marasova chuckles.

The snow turtle has pebbles for eyes and sea weed for legs. When it is finished the children lie down in the snow and flap their arms up and down to make angel wings before throwing snowballs at each other. Their fingers feel like they will drop off because they are so cold but Anji and Peter don't care because they are having such a great time.

'Today is so brilliant I shall remember it forever,' Peter says and Anji agrees.

It is nearly lunchtime, so they start climbing the steps, very carefully.

'I wish snow was warm,' Peter says.

'Warm and pink would be even better,' Anji says.

'When it gets warm and the snow turtle melts, does it mean he's died?' Peter asks.

Anji says, very slowly,

'Peter, that snow turtle is not alive or real.'

And Peter thinks for a moment then he says,

'Does that mean he is dead then?'

And Anji says,

'Peter, the snow turtle has never been alive so it cannot die. People die, pets die. Snowmen and snow turtles don't because they are not alive.'

Peter is silent for a few seconds. Then he says,

'How do I know *I'm* not going to melt?'

'You will if you go on asking stupid questions.'

But they are not stupid to Peter.

'So will I melt?' he asks again.

''Course you won't,' she says.

'But the snowman will melt and disappear, won't he?'

And all Anji says is,

'Yes.'

■ Ask,

> What do you think you will remember about yourself when you grow up? Share ideas with the class.

■ In summary, say,

> We have thought about memories and how they can become even more important after someone has died. We have thought about what it's like when someone is seriously ill; it can be really tough for everyone but it is okay to find it tough. We've also thought about guilt because when Marasova was ill, Anji and Peter might have forgotten about the helpful things they did for him. And there is one more thing to remember. Nothing anyone says, and nothing anyone thinks, can cause someone to die.

■ Let children draw as they begin to process their thoughts.

4 CARING FOR EACH OTHER WHEN SOMEONE DIES

Children think about how a community might support people who are very ill and how we might feel after someone we know dies.

Preparation

It is important to be aware of any children who are bereaved so that you are prepared to respond appropriately to any comments they may make or reactions they may have.

Have paper ready to make a card for Anji and Peter.

- Revisit the ground rules. See if children can remember what they are.

    1   You don't have to share something if you feel it is too private.
    2   Listen carefully to each other.

> **TIP**
>
> Recapping the third rule is especially important today.

    3   After someone dies, some people feel very sad and other people might not feel anything at all. We're all different and it is okay not to feel the same as other people do.

- Today we are thinking about how people might support each other when someone is hurting.

> **TIP**
>
> In order to keep this lesson objective, when working with the whole class, keep the focus on the story rather than your personal experiences. Avoid sharing personal experiences.

- On whiteboards or paper, ask children to write a list of feelings talked about so far in the story.

- Quickly make a list on the board of their collective ideas, recapping events that led to each feeling.

- Read the first part of the story.

Mum helps Anji tidy her room – every cupboard, every box and every shelf. How boring is that?

'Don't take the doll's house to the charity shop,' Peter says. 'Marasova could live in it. It's even got a yellow front door.'

So Peter and Anji take the doll's house down to the beach.

'Thank you!' Marasova chuckles. 'Put it next to the shed. I shall enjoy living in it and you can leave chocolate cake for me on the balcony.'

But as soon as the children leave the beach, who should appear but . . . the mumin spluffs. They fly as close as they can to the house, squawking as they do.

'I knew they would be back,' Marasova sighs. 'And I know what is going to happen. They are flying too close to the house and one of them will . . .'

And one of them does. The baby gull flies straight into the roof, cartwheels over the top, then dribbles across the sand.

Next day, the house is full of a baby seagull.

'That house is for you, not a stupid little spluff,' Anji says.

'The gull is injured,' Marasova says, 'so I am looking after her until she is better. I've given her a name. She's called Dribble.'

'You gave . . . that spluff . . . a name?' Anji says.

And all Marasova does is chuckle and nod his head.

While Dribble's wing mends, Marasova becomes Dribble's friend. In fact, he becomes friends with all the gulls and gives them all names. They won't be nasty to him now and even agree to fly out to sea if they want to squawk loudly.

So they won't be dumping umpo on him again. Ever.

'I still want to be covered in polish though,' Marasova tells the children, 'because I like the shine it puts on my yellow shell, and I like the smell.'

The children laugh. They love this beach. One day they might even learn to love the spluffs.

Only they are not called spluffs anymore. They're called Dribble, Sybil, Fizzle, Wiggle and Chelsea.

■ Say,

> Last week we talked about what it might be like at home when someone is ill. When Marasova was ill, Anji and Peter tried to cheer him up by painting his shell.

> Dribble's wing is mending but can you think what it is like for someone who is not just a bit ill, but very, very ill for a long time and is not getting better?

■ Ask,

> What do people who are very ill do and what don't they do?

TIP

Keep this light: e.g., they don't go sand dancing or run the marathon. By having some lighter moments, children feel they are more in control of the lesson content. They do stay in bed, don't want to eat and sometimes even watching the telly is too much.

■ Draw a picture in the middle of a whiteboard or piece of paper of someone ill in bed. Then draw and label all the people who might be able to help that person.

> Share ideas with the class.

TIP

Make sure 'friends' are mentioned.

■ When children say doctors and nurses, say,

> Most of the time, doctors and nurses do make people better but sometimes people are too ill for the medicines to work.

■ Read the next part of the story.

Anji has a new pair of wellies. They are pink and she wants to show Marasova. Peter has the certificate Mr Hawkins gave him in assembly for scoring a goal in last week's football match.

It looks like Marasova is still asleep inside his house so Peter puts his certificate on the table in the shed and kicks the ball against the cliff wall for a few minutes. Anji paddles in the sea.

After a while she comes back to Marasova's house and pulls the front panel wide open. Gently, she slides her hand under his shell to lift him out.

His body is stone cold.

TIP

Keep reading as normal. If you normally read with lots of emotion and expression, possibly reduce the emotion.

Slowly she realises what has happened, but at that moment she doesn't want to believe it. And then she hears Peter's voice behind her saying,

'Is he awake yet?'

'Peter,' she says as calmly as she can, 'I think Marasova is dead.'

The words come out in a whisper and she starts to cry.

'No, he's not,' Peter says. 'He'll wake up in a minute.'

'Peter, he is dead,' Anji says again and her voice is trembling.

They love Marasova.

He is their friend.

Only now he is gone.

And it hurts inside.

They are both crying and it is okay to do that. Anji puts her arms round her little brother and hugs him.

She is remembering things like Marasova's chuckle and how he used to sit on top of sandcastles and waggle his legs.

She remembers when they thought he had been swept out to sea and how awful that was. And when they made snow turtles and he watched.

They looked after him when he was ill, bought polish with their pocket money and chocolate cupcakes for his birthday party.

Marasova helped Peter get better at football and had helped her with her spellings.

But he will not do that anymore.

Peter kneels down and picks up two pebbles that are lying next to Marasova's house. One is blue and the other one is pink.

'It's like . . . it's like Marasova left us a present,' he whispers.

Anji stares at the pebbles and remembers how they used to paint them all different colours. She imagines she can hear Marasova talking to her now in his deep voice. But all Anji can really hear are the gulls high in the sky and Peter's breathing.

'We must go home and tell Mum and Dad,' she says. 'And . . . and I want to tell Marasova about my pink wellies. Even though he is dead, I can still write him a letter.'

'If you put your letter in an envelope,' Peter whispers, 'can we paint it bright yellow and can I put my football certificate in it as well?'

Anji nods and hugs her little brother once more. They are in this together. Then they turn and their footprints leave a trail in the sand as together they slowly walk towards the cliff steps.

TIP

This next activity is designed to be an opportunity for children to start processing what the story is about. Go straight on to it without a break after finishing the story.

■ Say,

> Over the last few weeks, the feelings we have thought about, many of which are on the board, are feelings Anji and Peter might have after Marasova has died.

> Remember the ground rules each week? We are all different and Anji and Peter might feel all of the feelings or just some of them.

■ Ask children to think of four or five feelings Anji and Peter might be feeling right now when they have just found out that Marasova is dead. There are no right or wrong answers.

> Stand up and find a friend to share your chosen feelings

TIP

Moving around will relieve tension. If some children are crying, reassure them that this is okay because the story is sad. Then encourage them to join in the activity.

■ Ask,

> What do you think someone who did not know Marasova might feel about him dying?

■ In pairs, ask children to write down one or two things they might do to help if someone who is important to one of their friends died. Then read out some of the list below. If the children have similar things, they can tick them off.

1 Be a good friend (explore what this means and refer back to the ground rules of listening and not having to share things that are too private).

2 Share some sweets with them.

3 Let them sit next to you.

4 Listen to what they are saying.

5 If you don't feel sad, you don't have to pretend you are.

6 If you are not the person's best friend, don't suddenly pretend you are.

7 Treat the person normally but remember they might be feeling a bit wobbly at times.

8 Invite them to your house to watch a DVD or play on the PlayStation.

9 Just keep being there for them but make sure you have other friends to be with as well.

10 Go to a football match with them.

11 Talk to them about the person who has died.

12 Hang out with them like you usually do.

13 Do something with them and include a few other people as well.

■ Say,

> If it is someone's birthday we send cards to let them know we are thinking about them. We do the same if someone dies. We're going to design a card to send to Peter and Anji to let them know that we are thinking about them because a friend of theirs (Marasova) has died.

> Hand out paper and write the words Anji, Peter and Marasova on the board. This is a time to chat to children as they draw.

TIP

If asked about funerals, explain that it is a special ceremony to say 'good-bye' to someone who has died. People do different things, depending on what they believe, or whether they have a religious faith.

■ In summary, say,

> Today we've thought about what we and other people might do to help someone who is very, very ill. Sadly, not everyone who is ill gets better because sometimes they are too unwell for medicines to work. We've thought about how we might feel after someone we know dies and how we might help a friend if someone important to them has died.

TIP

The activity may have stirred up difficult feelings in some children so it is essential to reassure all the class and remind those who feel they need it where to go for support.

All life has a beginning and an ending; it is part of the life cycle. Most people die when they are old but sadly some die when they are young. It is okay to talk about people who have died, or who are dying. Remember, in school there are people who will listen to you if there is anything you want to talk about, no matter what it is.

■ On paper or whiteboards, let children draw anything they want to.

For children aged 5–7

1 THE BEACH, THE CHILDREN AND THE TURTLE

Children think about special places, special people and people, their feelings and the wishes they make.

Throughout, the term 'children' refers to those listening to and interacting with the story. The children in the story text are referred to as Peter and Anji.

Preparation

Download pictures of (in this order) . . . an unpopulated beach, a seagull, steps leading down a cliff face to a beach, a blue and yellow blow-up dinghy with oars, a foot pump to inflate the dinghy, a turtle, a storm, a chocolate cupcake (if possible with a birthday candle on it).

If you think your children need a 3D representation of the beach/setting, details of how to do this are on pages 108–110 and in Appendices A and B.

■ Explain that this story is about feelings, including feelings we might have after someone has died. To help children feel safe, certain ground rules need to be talked about. These are repeated each week.

1 You don't have to share something if you feel it is too private.
2 Listen carefully to each other.
3 After someone dies, some people feel very sad and other people might not feel anything at all. We're all different and it is okay not to feel the same as other people do.

> **TIP**
>
> Phrases and concepts that need careful wording or explanation are written so they can be used directly from the script. These are indicated by the word 'Ask' or 'Say' written on a line with the question or comment on the line below.

■ Look at a picture of an empty beach on the whiteboard.

Ask children what else could be added to it. Use this to introduce beach vocabulary, including seagulls, cliffs with steps, blue and yellow dinghies with oars and a foot pump (to inflate the dinghy).

■ Read the first part of the story.

Peter and Anji carefully walk down the steps. The steps lead to their own little beach which is at the bottom of their garden.

Mum is in front of them, helping Dad carry a huge cardboard box. Inside the box are two oars, a foot pump and a yellow and blue blow-up dinghy. The dinghy is a present from Granny.

When they reach the sand, Dad uses the foot pump to blow air into the dinghy.

Then he says to Mum, 'You take the boat out first, with Anji.'

'What are you going to do while we are on the water?' Mum asks.

'You'll find out,' is all Dad will say.

He is planning something, but Mum does not know what.

Dad and Peter help Anji and Mum into the boat. Gulls swoop and fly above them as Mum and Anji pull on the oars to make the front of the boat cut through the water.

Dad and Peter turn round and walk back up the beach towards the cliffs.

'Let's be busy!' Dad says and Peter starts giggling.

A few minutes later Mum says,

'Look what Dad and Peter are doing!'

Anji looks back towards the beach.

Her mouth drops open.

She cannot believe what she can see.

■ Ask children what they think Dad and Peter are doing on the beach.

Back on the beach, Dad and Peter are painting a goal post on the cliff face. It is a bright blue goal post.

'We've got to go back and stop them!' Mum shouts. 'They cannot do that.'

But they can.

And they have.

'Don't worry,' Dad says, 'the paint will wear off in a few months. It won't be on the cliffs for ever.'

Mum then starts laughing because the blue goal post lines are all wiggly and Dad has blue paint on his nose and on his chin and on his shorts and on his fingers.

Anji starts laughing too. Not in a nasty way, but because she knows that the beach and her family are very, very special.

■ What different feelings do the family feel in the story?

■ The beach is Anji and Peter's favourite place and they go there with their favourite people. Ask children to tell their partner where their favourite place is and who their favourite people are.

Share their answers with the rest of the class and say how they feel in their favourite place.

TIP

Children could draw their favourite place and the people they like to go there with. If they do this, don't spend more than five minutes on this activity.

■ Look at pictures of a turtle, a storm and a chocolate cupcake (if possible with a birthday candle on it).

■ Read the next part of the story.

Marasova arrives on the beach one day after a storm.

'Hello,' he says in a croaky voice, 'I am very pleased to meet you.'

Peter and Anji stare at him and the weird thing is they both understand what he says.

'Where have you come from?' Peter asks him.

'The Big Sea,' Marasova says. 'I came here to shelter from the storm but this beach is a lovely place for a turtle to live. Can I stay here?'

Of course he can!

'He must have a date for his birthday,' Mum says.

'And a chocolate birthday cake,' Dad adds.

No one knows when Marasova's real birthday is. October 1st is the next time the children go to the beach, so they decide that October 1st will be his birthday. They have a birthday party for him and wear fancy dress.

■ Ask children what dressing up clothes they would wear if they went to Marasova's party on the beach.

'Marasova, how old do you want to be?' Peter asks.

'Seven,' he says. 'Then I am one year older than you and one year younger than your sister.'

'Make a wish,' Peter says as Marasova blows out the seven candles on his birthday cake.

'My shell is grey and I wish it was bright yellow,' he laughs. 'But my shell will never change, because it can't.'

'Marasova, you're not meant to tell anyone what you wish!' Anji says.

'I didn't know that,' Marasova says. Then he laughs and thanks the children for his birthday cake. He has never had one before.

Neither has the big fat seagull that suddenly swoops down, sticks its beak into the swirly chocolate sugar icing and takes off again with the cake hanging from its beak.

'Oy!' Peter shouts at the seagull. 'Give that back!' But all the seagull does is drop a sticky splat of poo right in front of Peter's left foot.

'Stupid seagull,' Peter shouts at it, 'you nearly hit me.'

■ Ask children what, in the story, could and could not happen in real life.

> **TIP**
>
> Marasova does NOT morph into other things or do magic tricks. He talks and knows about Anji and Peter's life but is still semi-constrained by physical things a turtle can and cannot do. He also has feelings.

- Ask what wishes children have made when they have blown out candles on a birthday cake or at another time. Have any of them come true?

- Ask children to draw a picture (on whiteboards or paper) of a wish they have made and, if appropriate, write the wish underneath.

- Ask children to tell a partner about the feelings they felt when they made the wish.

- In summary, say,

    Today we have thought about feelings and wishes.

    Sometimes we feel happy, sometimes sad and sometimes . . . *say other feelings mentioned during the lesson*. These are feelings everyone has and we are learning about them; even when we get older, we will still be learning about them.

    Wishes are important too; sometimes they can come true and sometimes they can't.

- Let children draw anything they like from the story so far. This is to give them time to start processing what has been thought about during the lesson.

2 FOOTBALL TEAMS, BUILDING SANDCASTLES AND LOSING MARASOVA

Children think about their response to things they cannot control. One possible response is anger. They then think how they might feel when someone important to them has gone.

Preparation

Download pictures of . . . building sandcastles, fighting the tide, life jackets and marker buoys. Add these to last week's pictures.

Write the word HAPPY on a piece of paper or whiteboard and ANGRY on another. Have felt tipped pens and more paper or whiteboards ready.

■ Ask children what they remember from the story last time. Use last week's pictures to jog memories.

■ Revisit the ground rules.

1 You don't have to share something if you feel it is too private.
2 Listen carefully to each other.
3 After someone dies, some people feel very sad and other people might not feel anything at all. We're all different and it is okay not to feel the same as other people do.

■ Say,

Today we are thinking about how we might feel when things happen that we cannot control – such as when it rains all day. We are also thinking about how we might feel if someone or something that is important to us goes missing.

■ Look at pictures of children building sandcastles and fighting the tide. Make sure children understand what these are.

■ Read the next part of the story.

'I wish I was better at football,' Peter says.

'If you like, I will help you get better,' Marasova says, 'but not today because I want to build a sandcastle and try and stop the tide knocking it down.'

The sandcastle they build is enormous and when it is finished, Anji and Peter lift Marasova on top of it. He chuckles and waggles his legs in the air.

Marasova stays there until the tide comes in and the water starts knocking the sandcastle down. Then he slides into the water and swims out to sea; the children jump on what is left of the castle. As they do, Peter bumps into Anji. It is an accident but Anji thinks he did it on purpose.

'Oy!' she shouts at him. 'Why did you do that?'

Then she pushes him and he falls over.

'You're little, you're weak,' she says.

He hates it when Anji is nasty to him and makes him feel small.

'I'm not little,' he shouts.

'Oh yes you are,' she says.

'I'm not weak either,' he yells.

'Oh yes you are. And you're pathetic. And you're probably going to cry now as well.'

And Peter hurts inside because his best friend, Ahmed, is really good at football and is big and strong. Ahmed is taller and stronger than Peter is as well.

Suddenly Peter hates everybody, especially Anji, and high above, seagulls squawk and he thinks they are laughing at him too because he is so small and useless and cannot do anything about it.

- Ask a child to come to the front and hold up the word HAPPY. Ask another to hold up the word ANGRY. Can children think of feelings words that go in between these two? Write each new feeling on a piece of paper or whiteboard and ask a child to stand where they think it would go in the feeling line.

TIP

Use this as an opportunity to reinforce that people see things differently.

- Introduce some angry words to show there are different strengths to the emotion, such as . . . *cross, annoyed, sad, upset, miserable.*

- Ask,

    Like Peter, when have you really wanted to do something and not been able to? Which of these feelings did you have?

- Not being in control made Peter angry. How did it make him behave?

- Ask children to make angry faces and then stand up and make angry poses with their bodies.

- Ask,

    How do you help yourself when you are feeling angry?

- Look at pictures of the dinghy (from last week), life jackets and marker buoys.

- Read the next part of the story.

When the children take the dinghy out on the water, Marasova loves lying on the front of it. Behind him, Peter and Anji sit side by side in their life jackets, one oar each, rowing towards the orange markers which are as far as they are allowed to row. It is dangerous if they go past the orange markers as they might be swept out into the Big Sea.

Peter turns round to wave at Marasova.

But Marasova is not there.

'Where is he?' Peter asks.

'He'll have dropped into the sea and gone for a swim,' Anji says. But Peter shakes his head.

'Marasova always lets us know where he is,' Peter says. 'Has he fallen off the boat and got trapped underneath it?'

They both look into the deep swirling sea.

'Has he swum out past the orange markers to the Big Sea?' Peter asks.

'I don't know,' Anji says.

'Should we row out and have a look?' Peter says.

'No,' Anji says straight away. 'Mum and Dad have said we must never go past the orange markers.'

'How strong are Marasova's legs?' Peter asks.

'He'll be all right,' Anji says quickly and is pleased her voice doesn't show how worried she is.

Then Peter says, 'If Marasova is dragged out to the Big Sea, how can Mum and Dad find him again?'

And all Anji says is, 'They can't.'

Then she says, 'Let's row back to the beach.'

'Marasova's gone, hasn't he?' Peter whispers. 'He's gone back to the Big Sea. Did he go back because we argued with each other?'

All Anji says is, 'I don't know.'

The children drag the dinghy onto the beach.

'We'd better tell Mum and Dad,' Anji says.

'Tell them what?' a voice says behind them.

Both children spin round.

A turtle looks up at them with a big grin on his wrinkled face.

'I've had a great swim,' he says.

'But we've been so worried,' Anji says. 'We didn't know where you were.'
'I went for a swim,' the turtle says.

But suddenly the sun is shining and everyone is smiling and Peter's heart stops hurting.

■ Ask,

> Have you ever lost something and been really worried about it?
>
> Tell either a partner or the class about it.

TIP

If children cannot think of anything, they can draw Peter and Anji when they realised Marasova was not in the boat with them.

■ In summary, say,

> Today we have thought about how things happen and we cannot always control them. It might make us feel angry. It could also make us feel scared and helpless, especially if something or someone who is really important goes missing.

■ Let children draw anything they like from the story so far. This is to give them time to start processing what has been thought about during the lesson.

3 SEVEN DAYS AND THEN MARASOVA IS PAINTED

Children think about grandparents, when someone is ill, what might make us feel guilty and the importance of memories.

Preparation

Download pictures of home-made biscuits. Find a picture of a grandparent wearing false teeth. If possible, bring in furniture polish to show the children.

- Revisit the ground rules.

    1   You don't have to share something if you feel it is too private.
    2   Listen carefully to each other.
    3   After someone dies, some people feel very sad and other people might not feel anything at all. We're all different and it is okay not to feel the same as other people do.

- Recap the story by looking at the pictures from the previous two sessions and then at the biscuits and false teeth. What do children think today's story will be about?

- Today we are thinking about grandparents, what happens when someone is ill and what might make us feel guilty.

Before Anji and Peter visit Granny they find pebbles and shells on the beach and paint them. The pink shells are Anji's, the yellow ones are Marasova's and the blue ones are Peter's.

At Granny's they make biscuits and watch her take out her false teeth and put them in a glass. She often talks to Grandad's picture on top of the television as well. He died two years ago.

'I still miss him,' Granny says. 'Do you remember the noise his motorbike used to make?'

Anji does.

It was very loud.

Anji and Peter miss their grandad too. He used to play football and cards with them and send them emails with funny pictures on that he downloaded from the internet.

- Ask children what their grandparents do with them.

> **TIP**
>
> If children have never known grandparents, let them draw pictures of things they have done with another relative or family friend. If children talk about grandparents who have died, let them share what they are comfortable sharing.

- On whiteboards or paper, ask children to draw a picture of something they have done with their grandparents.

- Share their pictures.

- Say,

  You have memories of your grandparents. After they and other important people and pets die, these will become really important. No one can ever take memories away. They will always be there to treasure.

- Ask children if they have a grandparent who . . . wears fluffy slippers . . . has a beard . . . likes eating tomato soup . . . is kind to them.

TIP

This is a deliberately 'light' activity.

- Read the next part of the story.

On Sunday, as soon as they return home from Granny's, Anji and Peter go to the beach. It is a good thing they do because Marasova is ill.

Peter and Anji find a towel in the shed and wrap him up in it.

'We'll look after you,' Anji whispers and lifts Marasova into her arms and carries him across the beach and up the steps.

'He needs to be where we can help him,' she says.

Mum makes a special place for Marasova in the garage. He stays there for seven whole days and sleeps most of the time. A lot happens that week.

MONDAY: Anji and Peter go to the cinema after school and Mum buys them a big box of popcorn to eat.

TUESDAY: Peter goes to judo club for the first time and really enjoys it.

WEDNESDAY: Peter has saved his pocket money for eight weeks so now has enough money to buy a new kite.

THURSDAY: It rains all day and the road to their house is flooded.

FRIDAY: Anji gets a good work certificate in assembly for writing a story about a cat with a curly tail.

SATURDAY: It is windy so the children visit the beach to fly Peter's new kite and it is brilliant!

'I wish Marasova could be here to see this,' Peter says to Anji.
SUNDAY: Marasova whispers,
'I feel better today.'
And that is the best thing that happens all week.

■ On whiteboards or paper, ask children to draw someone who is ill.

TIP

Lots of these drawings will be of people vomiting. Enjoy these then highlight one that has someone lying in bed. Talk about how some people have illnesses that last a long time.

■ Ask,

> What might it be like to have someone at home who is unwell for a very long time?

■ Say,

> Sometimes, when people are very ill, they can be a bit grumpy because they are feeling so unwell.

■ Read the next part of the story.

The children want to cheer Marasova up after he goes back to the beach.
'You know Marasova wants to be bright yellow,' Peter says to Anji. 'Let's go down to the beach when he is asleep and paint his shell.'
'We'll have to go when it is dark,' Anji says.
Peter nods. That is partly why he thinks it is such a good idea.
So Anji finds some yellow paint and when Mum and Dad are watching the television, Anji and Peter tiptoe downstairs and out of the back door. Anji has a bag in her left hand and Dad's expensive torch in the other.

■ What are Peter and Anji wearing?

TIP

Elaborate on pyjamas and nighties having interesting motifs and patterns, such as frogs and football club badges. This is deliberately 'light' after thinking about illness.

It is dark and little bit spooky, walking in the moonlight. When they reach the gate at the top of the cliff steps, Anji suddenly grabs Peter's left hand.

'I thought you might fall over the cliff,' she says.

'You didn't,' Peter whispers. 'You are scared.'

'I am not!' she says, letting go of his hand.

They find Marasova near the shed. He is asleep. Anji passes the torch to Peter.

'Do not drop it,' she whispers. 'It's Dad's torch and don't get sand in it.' He holds it very tightly making sure no light shines on Marasova's face in case it wakes him up.

Anji opens her bag and takes out two paintbrushes and some yellow paint.

'We need some water,' she whispers, 'let's go to the shed to get a bucket.'

When they reach the shed door, Peter thinks Anji is just behind him so he turns round to whisper something to her. But she has disappeared.

Peter stands still. His heart is beating extra fast. He can't call out or he might wake Marasova.

Anji must be hiding behind the shed. He shines Dad's torch on the ground and walks right round the shed.

But Anji isn't there.

He is on his own.

On the beach.

And it is dark and he is frightened.

'Anji!' Peter whispers, 'where are you?'

'Who's scared now?' a voice whispers and Anji jumps out from behind the shed.

'I looked behind the shed,' Peter whispers. 'I walked all round it.'

'I know you did. You shone the torch in front of you so I knew when you were coming. You're the scared chicken now!'

'I am not!' he says and swallows hard to stop himself crying.

'Come on!' Anji says. 'Let's be quick, do the painting and go back to bed.'

She is suddenly feeling guilty about borrowing Dad's torch without asking. She should not have done it.

And maybe she should not have hidden from Peter and scared him so much.

And then she feels guilty again because Mum and Dad don't know where she and Peter are. Peter and Anji always have to tell them if they are going to the beach.

She is meant to be more sensible than Peter because she is older than he is. She wishes she had left a note on her pillow saying where they were.

'We must be extra sensible,' she says to Peter who nods because he knows he is already being extra sensible.

TIP

Developmentally, children do not begin to understand what guilt is until they are 6–7 years old. If working with younger children, miss the following activity out and go straight on to the next part of the story.

- Ask,

    How might guilt make you feel inside?

- Say,

    Guilt is feeling bad because you think you have made something nasty happen. Anji has frightened Peter and might have made Mum and Dad very cross because she took Dad's torch.

- Ask,

    Peter and Anji had a great week when Marasova was ill. Do you think they might have felt guilty about it afterwards? Why? Why not?

    What do you do when someone is ill?

TIP

Many children feel guilty when someone is ill and blame themselves. It is good to remind children to think of something they have done that is positive, such as making a card or visiting them or keeping quiet. This might help them feel less guilty.

■ Read the next part of the story.

___

Next morning, Peter and Anji go to the beach, but Marasova is hiding behind the shed.

'What's wrong?' Anji asks. 'Don't you like your shell?'

'I love it,' Marasova whispers. 'But the gulls keep dropping poo on me!'

'They what?'

'They keep dropping poo on me.'

'Stupid seagulls!' Peter shouts.

'Sometimes,' Marasova says quietly, 'something happens and you cannot do anything about it. Like this. The gulls will never change. They are just a pain in the neck. You'd better paint me grey again, but thank you for trying. It was such a lovely idea.'

And then Peter says,

'If we put polish on your shell, the poo would slide off it.'

What a brilliant idea!

TIP

Make sure children understand this is furniture polish, which is slippery, and not shoe polish.

So next time the seagulls drop poo on Marasova, it does not stick to his shell. Instead, it slides off and onto the sand.

'We won!' Peter shouts at the seagulls.

A few weeks later, beautiful cold snowflakes fall and cover everything. School is closed so the children put on their wellies and their coats and hats and scarves and take chocolate cake and sardines to the beach.

'Everyone else builds snowmen,' Anji says, 'but we are going to make a snow turtle.'

'And I shall watch you from the shed,' Marasova chuckles.

When the snow turtle is finished the children lie down in the snow and flap their arms up and down to make angel wings before throwing snowballs at each other.

'Today is so brilliant I want to remember it forever,' Peter says.

'I wish snow was warm,' Peter says.

'Warm and pink would be better,' Anji says.

'That snow turtle will melt soon, won't it?' Peter says. 'Does that mean it's dead?'

And Anji says,

'Peter, the snow turtle has never been alive so it cannot die. People die, pets die. Snowmen and snow turtles don't because they are not alive.'

'Will I melt when we go home?' Peter says.

''Course you won't,' she says and they both laugh.

- Ask children to tell their partner one thing they have done that they can remember.

- In summary, say,

  > We have thought about memories and how they can be really precious, especially if someone, or a pet, has died. Then we looked at what it's like when someone is seriously ill; it can be difficult for everyone and it is okay to find it difficult.

  > We have also thought about feeling guilty and thinking something is our fault. If someone is ill or if someone dies, it won't be your fault. Nothing you say or think can make anyone die.

- Let children draw as they begin to process their thoughts.

4 CARING FOR EACH OTHER WHEN SOMEONE DIES

Children think about how a community might support people who are very ill and how we night feel after someone we know dies.

Preparation

It is important to be aware of any children who have recently been bereaved so you can respond appropriately to comments they make.

Have paper ready to make a card for Anji and Peter.

- Revisit the ground rules.

  1 You don't have to share something if you feel it is too private.
  2 Listen carefully to each other.

TIP

Recapping the third rule is especially important today.

3 After someone dies, some people feel very sad and other people might not feel anything at all. We're all different and it is okay not to feel the same as other people do.

■ Today we are thinking about how people might support each other when someone is hurting.

TIP

In order to keep this lesson objective, when working with the whole class, avoid sharing personal experiences.

■ On the board, write a list of feelings talked about in the story so far – right back to the first lesson. The list will be needed at the very end of the lesson.

■ Read the next part of the story.

Mum helps Anji tidy her room – every cupboard, every box and every shelf.

'Marasova could live in the doll's house,' Peter says. 'It's even got a yellow front door.'

So Peter and Anji carefully carry the doll's house to the beach.

'Thank you!' Marasova chuckles. 'Put it next to the shed. I shall enjoy living in it.'

But as soon as the children leave the beach, who should appear but . . . the seagulls. They fly as close as they can to the house, squawking loudly as they do.

'I knew they would be back,' Marasova sighs. 'And I know what is going to happen. They are flying too close to the house and one of them will . . .'

And one of them does. The baby gull flies straight into the roof, cartwheels over the top, then dribbles across the sand.

Next day, the house is full of a baby seagull.

'That house is for you, not a gull,' Anji tells Marasova.

'The gull is injured,' Marasova says, 'so I am looking after her until she is better. I've given her a name. She's called Dribble.'

'You gave . . . that seagull . . . a name?' Anji says.

And Marasova chuckles and nods his head.

While Dribble's wing mends, Marasova becomes her friend. In fact, he becomes friends with all the gulls and gives them all names. They won't be nasty to him now and even agree to fly out to sea if they want to squawk loudly.

'I still want to be covered in polish though,' Marasova tells the children, 'because I like the shine it puts on my yellow shell, and I like the smell.'

Anji and Peter laugh. They love this beach. One day they might even learn to love the gulls. Only they are not called gulls anymore. They're called Dribble, Sybil, Fizzle, Wiggle and Chelsea.

■ Say,

> Last week we talked about what it might be like when someone is ill. When Marasova was ill, Anji and Peter tried to cheer him up. How?

> Dribble's wing is mending but can you think what it is like for someone who is not just a bit ill, but very, very ill for a long time and is not getting better?

■ Ask,

> What do people who are very ill do and what don't they do?

TIP

Keep this light – e.g., they don't go sand dancing or run the marathon. By including lighter moments, children feel they are more in control of the lesson content. They do stay in bed, don't want to eat and sometimes even watching the telly is too much.

■ Draw a picture in the middle of a whiteboard or piece of paper of someone ill in bed. Then draw all the people who might be able to help that person.

Share ideas.

■ When children say doctors and nurses, say,

> They do make people better but sometimes people are too ill for the medicines to work so they don't get better.

■ Read the next part of the story.

Anji has a new pair of pink wellies. She wants to show Marasova and Peter wants to show him his certificate because he has improved so much at playing football.

It looks like Marasova is still asleep inside his house so Peter puts his certificate on the table in the shed and kicks the ball against the cliff wall for a few minutes. Anji paddles in the sea to try out her new wellies.

After a while she comes back to Marasova's house and pulls the front panel wide open. Gently, she slides her hand under his shell to lift him out.

His body is stone cold.

She knows what has happened, but at that moment she doesn't want to believe it. And then she hears Peter's voice behind her saying,

'Is he awake yet?'

'Peter,' she says as calmly as she can, 'Marasova is dead.'

The words come out in a whisper.

'No he's not,' Peter says. 'He'll wake up in a minute.'

'Peter, he's dead,' Anji says again.

They are both crying. Anji puts her arms round her little brother and hugs him. She is remembering things like Marasova's chuckle and how he used to sit on top of a sandcastle and waggle his legs. She remembers when they thought he had gone back to the Big Sea and when they made snow turtles and he watched. They looked after him when he was ill and bought polish with their pocket money and chocolate cupcakes for his birthday party. He'd helped Peter get better at football. He had helped her with her spellings.

But he would not do that anymore.

Peter suddenly kneels down and picks up two pebbles that are lying next to the shed. One is blue and the other one is pink.

'It's like . . . it's like Marasova left us a present,' he whispers.

Anji stares at the pebbles. She imagines she can hear Marasova talking to her now in his deep voice. But all Anji can really hear are the gulls high in the sky.

'We must go home and tell Mum and Dad,' she says. 'And . . . and I want to write a letter and tell Marasova about my pink wellies.'

'If you put your letter in an envelope,' Peter whispers, 'can we paint it bright yellow and can I put my football certificate in it as well?'

Anji nods and hugs her little brother once more. They are in this together. Then they turn and their footprints leave a trail in the sand as together they walk slowly towards the cliff steps.

TIP

This next activity is designed to be an opportunity for children to start processing what the story is about. Go straight on to it without a break after finishing the story.

■ Say,

> The feelings on the board are feelings Anji and Peter might have felt after Marasova died. Remember the ground rules each week? We are all different and Anji and Peter might feel all of the feelings or just some of them.

■ Ask children to stand up and all together read the feelings out loud.

TIP

Doing this will relieve tension. If some children are crying, reassure them that this is okay because the story is sad. Then encourage them to join in the activity.

■ Ask,

> How would someone who did not know Marasova feel about him dying?

TIP

Refer back to the ground rules if need be; everyone reacts differently.

■ Ask children what we might do if someone who is important to one of our friends dies. Read some of the list below and see what children think about each one.

1 Be a good friend (explore what this means and refer back to the ground rules of listening and not having to share things that are too private).

2 Share some sweets with them.

3 Let them sit next to you.

4 Listen carefully to what they are saying.

5 If you don't feel sad, don't pretend you are.

6 Remember they might feel very sad.

TIP

Pretending is not helpful. Someone who is bereaved needs people to be honest.

7 Watch a DVD with them.

8 Go to a football match with them.

9 Talk to them about the person who has died.

10 Hang out with them like you usually do.

11 Do something with them and include a few other people as well.

- Say,

  > If it is someone's birthday we send cards to let them know we are thinking about them. We do the same if someone dies. We're going to make a card for Peter and Anji as if we are letting them know we are thinking about them. Hand out paper and let children design their card. If appropriate, this is a time to chat to children as they draw.

TIP

If asked about funerals, explain that it is a special ceremony to say 'good-bye' to someone who has died. People do different things, depending on what they believe, whether they have a religious faith, or whether they believe a person goes to an afterlife when they die.

- In summary, say,

  > Today we've thought about when someone is very, very ill and we've thought about what we might feel after someone dies and how we might help a friend if someone important to them dies. All life has a beginning and an ending. Most people die when they are old but sadly some die when they are young. It is okay to talk about people who have died, or who are dying. Remember, in school there are people who will listen to you if there is anything you want to talk about, no matter what it is.

TIP

The activity may have stirred up difficult feelings in some children so it is essential to reassure all the class and remind those who feel they need it where to go for support.

- On paper or whiteboards, let children draw anything they want to.

For children who speak English as a second language

1 THE BEACH, THE CHILDREN AND THE TURTLE

Children think about special places, special people, feelings and wishes they make. Throughout, the term 'children' refers to those listening to and interacting with the story. The children in the text are referred to as Peter and Anji.

Preparation

Download pictures of (in this order) a) empty beach, b) steps leading down a cliff face to a beach, c) a blue and yellow blow-up dinghy with oars, d) foot pump to inflate the dinghy, e) a seagull, f) a turtle, g) a storm, h) a chocolate cupcake (if possible with a birthday candle on it). More pictures will be added each session.

Making the beach out of a shoe box may be appropriate. If so, look at ideas given on pages 108–110 and in Appendices A and B.

- Explain that this story is about feelings, including feelings we might have after someone has died. To help the children feel safe, certain ground rules need to be talked about.

    1   You don't have to share something if you feel it is too private.
    2   Listen carefully to each other.
    3   After someone dies, some people feel very sad and other people might not feel anything at all. We're all different and it is okay not to feel the same as other people do.

> **TIP**
>
> Phrases and concepts that need careful wording or explanation are written so they can be used directly from the script. These are indicated by the word 'Ask' or 'Say' written on a line with the question or comment on the line below.

■ Talk about pictures of a deserted beach, steps leading down a cliff face to a beach, a blue and yellow blow-up dinghy with oars, a foot pump to inflate the dinghy and seagulls so that children can access the story.

■ Read the first part of the story.

There is a beach at the bottom of Peter and Anji's garden.
They are there today.
Mum and Dad are with them.
They have a large box. In it are two oars, a foot pump and a yellow and blue dinghy.
Dad says,
'Anji and Mum must go in the boat first.'
Seagulls fly in the sky. They sqquuuaaaaark as they fly. Mum helps Anji pull on the oars and the boat goes through the water.
A beach in your garden is good.
A beach with a boat is brilliant.

■ How is Anji feeling as she rows the boat with her mum on the sea?

Then Mum says,
'Look at Peter and Dad!'
Anji looks. Peter and Dad are painting on the cliff wall.
'We must stop them!' Mum shouts.

■ Ask children what they think Dad and Peter are painting on the cliffs.

Anji and Mum row back to the beach.

Dad smiles. He likes the blue goal post he and Peter have painted.

'The paint will disappear soon,' Dad says.

Mum looks cross. Then she starts laughing because the blue goal post has wiggly lines and Dad has blue paint on his nose and on his chin. Peter has blue paint on his nose.

Then Anji starts laughing too because she knows that the beach and her Mum and her Dad and her little brother are very, very special.

■ On whiteboards or paper, draw a picture of the beach with a shed, a dinghy boat on the sea, a seagull, shells, a blue goal post, a house where the children live, the cliff face with steps, gate, fence and sand.

■ Ask children how the characters are feeling in the story. Make a list of their answers on the board, drawing faces showing the emotion if appropriate.

■ The beach is Anji and Peter's favourite place. Ask children to draw themselves in their favourite place and add someone they like being with.

TIP

The wording of some questions has been thought about very carefully. These questions are laid out with 'Ask' on a line on its own with the question just below. Depending on the children's grasp of the language, adapt these questions as appropriate.

■ Look at pictures of a turtle so children know what one is; also the storm and the chocolate cupcake.

■ Then read the next part of the story.

Marasova is a turtle. He comes to the beach after a storm.

'Hello,' he says to the children.

Peter and Anji look at him. It is weird, but they understand what he says.

'Where are you from?' Peter asks him.

'The Big Sea,' Marasova says. 'I like this beach. It is a lovely place for a turtle to live.'

The children think Marasova must have a birthday. So they take a birthday cake to the beach. It is a chocolate cupcake with a candle on.

'Today is your birthday,' they say to Marasova.

'Thank you for my birthday cake,' he says.

■ Ask children what they have done at parties they have been to. How might a party on a beach be different?

Marasova blows out the candle on his cake and Anji says,

'When you blow out candles on a birthday cake, you make a wish.'

'What is a wish?' Marasova asks.

'A wish is when you want something to happen,' Anji says.

'I wish,' Marasova says slowly, 'that I was yellow.'

Then he says, 'I can never be yellow because my shell is grey. That wish will never come true.'

A big seagull flies down and picks up the chocolate birthday cake in his beak.

'Oy!' Peter shouts, 'give that back!'

But the gull does not give the cake back.

Instead, the gull drops white poo next to Peter's foot.

'Stupid seagull,' Peter shouts.

■ Ask children what, in the story, could and could not happen in real life.

TIP

Marasova does NOT morph into other things or do magic tricks. He talks and knows about Anji and Peter's life but is still semi-constrained by physical things a turtle can do. He also has feelings.

■ Ask children to draw a picture on whiteboards or paper of a want or a wish they have made. If appropriate, write about it underneath. Share their ideas with a partner and, using the list made earlier on the board, write the feelings they felt when they made it.

■ Say,

> Today we have thought about feelings such as when we feel happy, sad and . . . *say other feelings mentioned during the lesson*. These are feelings everyone has and we are learning about them. Wishes are important too; sometimes they come true and sometimes they don't.

■ Let children draw anything they like from the story so far. This is to give them time to start processing what has been thought about during the lesson.

2 FOOTBALL TEAMS, BUILDING SANDCASTLES AND LOSING MARASOVA

Children think about their response to things they cannot control. One possible response is anger. They then think how they might feel when someone important to them has gone.

Preparation

Download pictures of . . . building sandcastles, fighting the tide, life jackets and marker buoys. Add these to last week's pictures.

Draw a happy face and the word HAPPY on a piece of paper and draw an angry face and the word ANGRY on another. Have felt tipped pens and more paper ready.

■ On whiteboards or paper, ask children to draw one thing they remember from the story last time. Share their pictures with the class to recap what happened in the story.

■ Revisit the ground rules.

1 You don't have to share something if you feel it is too private.
2 Listen carefully to each other.
3 After someone dies, some people feel very sad and other people might not feel anything at all. We're all different and it is okay not to feel the same as other people do.

■ Look at pictures of children building sandcastles and fighting the tide, life jackets and marker buoys. Make sure children understand what each is and how it is used.

■ Today we are thinking about how we might feel when we have no control over something – like when it rains all day. We will also think about how we might feel if someone or something that is important to us is gone.

Then read the next part of the story.

Peter is angry. He wants to be in the school football team but he is not good enough.

'I will help you get better,' Marasova says. 'Kick the ball into the blue goal you and Dad painted on the cliff.'

Peter kicks the ball and misses the goal.

'You need to practise,' Marasova says.

Later, Peter and Anji build a big sandcastle. They want to stop the tide knocking it over. Peter puts Marasova on top of the sandcastle.

The waves knock the castle over. Marasova slides into the water and starts swimming.

Peter and Anji jump on the castle.

Peter jumps on Anji's foot.

It is an accident but Anji hits him.

Then she says,

'You are little and you are weak and . . .'

Peter is cross and kicks Anji. They both fall over.

'I am not little and I am not weak,' he shouts.

'Yes you are,' Anji says.

And Peter is sad because he wants to play in the school football team and Anji has made him feel like he can't do anything. Peter walks away.

He is crying and does not want Anji to see.

■ Ask a child to come to the front and hold the symbol/word HAPPY. Ask another to hold the symbol/word ANGRY. Can children think of feelings that go in between these two? Write or draw symbols for each new feeling on a piece of paper or whiteboard and ask a child to stand where they think it would go in the feelings line.

TIP

Use this as an opportunity to reinforce that people see things differently.

■ Make sure there are different strengths to the angry words such as . . . *cross, annoyed, sad, upset, miserable.*

■ Ask,

Like Peter, when have you wanted to do something and not been able to? How did it make you behave? Draw the time on whiteboards or paper. Choose a feeling to describe how you felt.

■ Think of several things children cannot change or control – e.g., *the weather, the date of their birthday, death, where they were born, having to learn English.* Make a list on the board, then ask children, in pairs, to decide which feeling they think is 'worst' and which is 'best'. Explain their choices.

■ On whiteboards or paper, ask children to draw what they think of when you say the word . . . 'anger'. Draw for about two minutes, then share what children have drawn.

■ Remind children they do not have to share anything they do not want to.

■ Ask,

Have you ever been nasty to someone because you were angry?

Share answers with a partner.

■ Ask,

How do you stop yourself feeling angry? Make a list of how, then look at pictures of life jackets and marker buoys.

■ Now read the next part of the story.

Marasova sits on the front of the blue and yellow dinghy. Peter and Anji row the boat out to sea.

They are wearing life jackets and row towards the orange markers. It is dangerous if they go past the orange markers because they might be pulled out to the Big Sea.

Peter turns round to look at Marasova.

But Marasova is not there.

'Where is he?' Peter asks.

'Marasova is swimming in the sea,' Anji says.

But Peter is worried.

'Marasova always lets us know where he is,' Peter says. 'Has he swum out past the orange markers?'

'I do not know,' Anji says.

'Shall we row out and look for him?' Peter says.

'No,' Anji says. 'Mum and Dad say we must never go past the markers.'

'Can turtles swim under the water?' Peter asks.

'Of course they can,' Anji says.

Then Peter says,

'If Marasova is in the Big Sea, can Mum and Dad find him?'

'No,' Anji says.

'I like Marasova living on our beach,' Peter says. 'Has he gone back to the Big Sea because we were nasty to each other?'

And Anji says,

'I do not know.'

Anji and Peter row back to the beach. They are feeling very sad.

The gulls squawk as Peter and Anji pull the dinghy out of the water and onto the sand.

'We must tell Mum and Dad,' Anji says.

'Why did Marasova go?' Peter says.

'I do not know,' Anji says.

She looks at the sea and suddenly there is Marasova, swimming towards the beach. He has a big smile on his face.

'I had a great swim,' he says.

'We thought you had gone back to the Big Sea,' Anji says.

'I wouldn't do that,' Marasova says. 'I like your beach.'

■ Ask,

> Have you ever lost something and been really worried about it? Tell
> either a partner or the class about it.

TIP

If children cannot think of anything, they can draw Peter and Anji when
Marasova was not in the boat with them.

■ Say,

> Today we have thought about how when things happen we cannot
> always control them. It might make us feel angry. It could also make
> us feel scared and helpless, especially if something or someone who
> is really important goes missing.

3 SEVEN DAYS AND THEN MARASOVA IS PAINTED

Children think about grandparents, when someone is ill, what might make us feel
guilty and the importance of memories.

Preparation

Download pictures of home-made biscuits, gull poo, furniture polish, snow and
people building snowmen. Add these, in order, to previous pictures.

Bring in furniture polish to show the children. Find a picture of a grandparent
wearing false teeth as well.

■ Revisit the ground rules.

1 You don't have to share something if you feel it is too private.
2 Listen carefully to each other.
3 After someone dies, some people feel very sad and other people
   might not feel anything at all. We're all different and it is okay not to
   feel the same as other people do.

- Recap the story by looking at the pictures from the previous two sessions and then at the biscuits and false teeth. What do children think today's story will be about?

- Today we are thinking about grandparents, what happens when someone is ill and how that might make us feel guilty.

- Now read the next part of the story.

Anji and Peter visit their grandmother. They have painted some shells and give them to her. The pink shells are Anji's, the yellow shells are Marasova's and the blue shells are Peter's.

Granny helps them make chocolate biscuits. Grandad liked chocolate biscuits. Grandad died two years ago.

'I wish Grandad was still alive,' Granny says. 'I miss him. Do you remember the noise his motorbike made?'

Anji does.

Grandad's motorbike was very loud.

Anji misses Grandad too. He used to play football and sent them emails.

- Ask children what their grandparents do with them.

> **TIP**
>
> If children have never known grandparents, let them draw pictures of things they have done with another relative or family friend. If children talk about grandparents who have died, let them share what they are comfortable sharing.

- On whiteboards or paper, ask children to draw a picture of something they have done with their grandparents. Share their pictures.

- Say,

    You have good memories of your grandparents. After they die, these will become more important. No one can take memories away. They will always be there to treasure.

■ Ask children whether they have a grandparent who . . . wears fluffy slippers . . . has a beard . . . lives in another country . . . likes eating soup . . . is kind.

■ Then read the next part of the story.

When Anji and Peter get back from Granny's house, Anji and Peter go to the beach.

Marasova is ill.

'We will look after you,' Anji whispers and she picks the turtle up and carries him home.

Mum makes a special place for Marasova in the garage. He stays there for seven days. A lot happens that week.

MONDAY: Dad buys tickets so he and Peter can watch Chelsea play Wigan at football.

TUESDAY: Peter plays in the school football team.

WEDNESDAY: Anji and Peter go to the swimming pool after school with Mum.

THURSDAY: Mum is at work so Dad cooks a chicken curry for tea.

FRIDAY: Anji gets a good work certificate in assembly.

SATURDAY: Anji and Peter go to the beach. They build a big sandcastle. 'I wish Marasova was with us,' Peter says to Anji.

SUNDAY: Marasova says,

'I feel better today.'

And that is the best thing that happens all week.

■ On whiteboards or paper, ask children to draw someone who is ill. Share what they draw with a partner or the class.

■ Ask,

> What would it be like to have someone at home who is unwell for a long time?

■ Say,

> Sometimes, when people are very ill, they can be cross and grumpy because they feel so unwell. That can be difficult for those around them.

■ Check that children understand what the prepositions *behind*, *next to* and *in front of* mean. They are important in this next section of the story.

Peter wants to help Marasova feel happy because he has been ill.
Peter says,
'Let's go to the beach when Marasova is asleep and paint him bright yellow.'
Anji says,
'We will have to go when it is dark.'
Anji finds some yellow paint. When Mum and Dad are watching television, Anji and Peter go downstairs and out of the back door. Anji carries a bag and Dad's big torch.

■ What are Peter and Anji wearing?

TIP

Elaborate on pyjamas and nighties having interesting motifs and patterns, such as frogs and football club badges.

Peter is scared because it is dark. But he does not tell Anji.
Marasova is asleep near the shed. Anji gives the torch to Peter.
'Do not drop it,' she says.
Peter holds the torch; if the light goes on Marasova's face it will wake him up.
Anji opens her bag. Inside are two paintbrushes and the yellow paint.
'We need some water,' she says. 'We must go to the shed to get a bucket.'
Peter goes first.

When they reach the shed, Peter looks behind at Anji. But Anji is not there.

Where has Anji gone?

Peter stands still. If he calls out Anji's name, Marasova will wake up.

Peter is glad he has Dad's torch. He walks round the shed, but Anji is not there.

'Anji!' he says.

He is very scared.

'Anji, where are you? I don't like being on the beach when it is dark.'

'Are you scared?' Anji says and she jumps out from behind the shed.

Peter is very happy to see her.

'I looked behind the shed,' Peter says.

Anji says,

'You shone the torch in front of you so I knew where you were and kept hiding from you.'

Anji suddenly wishes she had not hidden because Peter was so very scared.

And she is feeling guilty because she never asked Dad if she could borrow his torch.

Then she feels guilty because Mum and Dad do not know where they are.

Anji is more sensible than Peter because she is ten years old and he is eight years old.

She wishes she had left a note on her bed saying where they were.

■ Ask children to say what guilt is.

■ Say,

> Guilt is feeling bad because you think you have made something nasty happen. Anji frightened Peter and might have made Mum and Dad cross because she took Dad's torch and didn't tell them she and Peter were going to the beach.

■ Ask,

> How does guilt make you feel inside?

■ What do children do when someone is ill?

TIP

Many children feel guilty when someone is ill and blame themselves. So it is good to remind children to find something they have done that is positive, such as making a card or visiting them or keeping quiet. This might help them feel less guilty.

- Show a picture of gull poo and polish, then suggest children make themselves comfortable for a longer section of the story.

Next morning, Peter and Anji go to the beach to see Marasova's yellow shell.

But Marasova is hiding behind the shed.

'What's wrong?' Anji asks.

Marasova says,

'The gulls can see me now and drop poo on me.'

'Stupid seagulls!' Peter shouts.

Marasova says,

'Some things happen and you cannot change them. We can never change the gulls. Paint me grey again.' Then he says, 'Thank you for trying. It was a lovely idea.'

Then Peter says,

'Why don't we use yellow polish?'

And Anji and Marasova laugh.

TIP

Make sure children understand this is furniture polish, which is slippery, and not shoe polish.

So the children cover Marasova in bright yellow polish.

Then he walks onto the sand and pulls his head and legs into his shell.

The seagulls see him and fly back.

Their poo does not stick to his shell because the polish makes it slide off.

Peter writes WE BEAT YOU in the sand.

■ Look at pictures of snow and snowmen so children understand what they
   are.

A few weeks later, it snows and is very cold. Anji and Peter take chocolate
cake to Marasova and make sure he is all right.

'We are going to make a snow turtle,' Anji says.

'And I will watch you,' Marasova says.

When the snow turtle is finished, Peter and Anji make snowballs and throw
them at each other. They have a great time.

'I shall remember today forever,' Peter says.

'So will I,' Anji says.

'I wish snow was warm,' Peter says.

'I wish snow was warm and pink,' Anji whispers.

'When the snow turtle gets warm it will melt,' Peter says. 'Is that like the
snow turtle has died?'

Anji says,

'Peter, that snow turtle is not alive. It is not real. People die, snowmen and
snow turtles don't.'

'How do I know I won't melt when I get warm again?' Peter says.

'Because people do not melt,' Anji says.

■ What can children remember about when they were very little?

■ Say,

> We have thought about memories and how they can be really
> precious, especially if someone or a pet has died. Then we looked at
> what it's like when someone is seriously ill; it can be difficult for
> everyone and it is okay to find it difficult. We have also thought about
> feeling guilty and thinking something is our fault. If someone is ill or if
> someone dies, it won't be your fault. Nothing you say or think can
> make anyone die.

■ Let children draw as they begin to process their thoughts.

4 CARING FOR EACH OTHER WHEN SOMEONE DIES

Children think about how a community might support people who are very ill and how we night feel after someone we know dies.

Preparation

It is important to be aware of any children who have recently been bereaved. Have paper ready to make a card for Anji and Peter.

■ Revisit the ground rules. See if children can remember what they are.

1 You don't have to share something if you feel it is too private.
2 Listen carefully to each other.
3 After someone dies, some people feel very sad and other people might not feel anything at all. We're all different and it is okay not to feel the same as other people do.

■ Today we are thinking about how people might support each other when someone is hurting.

TIP

In order to keep this lesson objective, when working with the whole class, avoid sharing personal experiences.

■ On whiteboards or paper, ask children to write a list of feelings talked about so far in the story.

■ Quickly make a list on the board of their collective ideas, recapping the events that led to each feeling. Then read the first part of the story.

Anji does not want her doll's house anymore.
So Peter and Anji carry the doll's house to the beach.
'Thank you!' Marasova says. 'Put it next to the shed.'
When Anji and Peter leave the beach, the seagulls come. They fly as close as they can to the doll's house. They squawk as they do. They fly very close. Then . . .

BOOF!!! The baby bird flies into the cliff.

Next day, the doll's house is full of a baby seagull.

'That house is for you, not a seagull,' Anji says to Marasova.

'The seagull hurt her wing,' Marasova says, 'so I am looking after her until she is better.'

While the seagull's wing mends, Marasova becomes Dribble's friend. Then he becomes friends with all the other seagulls. They stop being nasty to Marasova and say they will fly out to sea if they want to squawk.

So everyone is happy.

'I still want polish on my shell,' Marasova tells the children, 'because I like my yellow shell to shine and I like the smell.'

Peter and Anji laugh.

They love this beach.

■ Say,

> Last week we talked about what it might be like when someone is ill. Marasova was ill, so Anji and Peter tried to make him happy by painting his shell yellow. What would it be like for someone who is very, very ill, for a long time, and is not getting better?

■ Ask,

> What do people who are very ill do and what don't they do?

TIP

Keep this light – e.g., they don't go sand dancing or run the marathon. By having some lighter moments, children feel they are more in control of the lesson content. They do stay in bed, don't want to eat and even watching the telly is too much.

■ Draw a picture in the middle of a whiteboard or piece of paper of someone ill in bed. Then draw and label people who can help that person. Share ideas with the class.

TIP

Make sure 'friends' are mentioned.

- When children say doctors and nurses, say,

  Doctors and nurses make people better but sometimes people are too ill for the medicines to work.

- Read the next part of the story.

Anji has a new pair of pink wellies. She wants to show Marasova. Peter has a certificate because he scored a goal when he played in the school football team. He wants to show that to Marasova too. Marasova is asleep in the doll's house. Anji wants to wake him up. So she puts her hand under his shell to lift him out. Marasova's body is cold.

> **TIP**
>
> Keep reading as normal. If you normally read with lots of emotion and expression, possibly reduce the emotion.

Anji knows what has happened.
Then Peter says,
'Is Marasova awake yet?'
'Peter,' Anji says, 'Marasova is dead.'
Anji is crying. They love Marasova. He is their friend.
Only now he has died. And it hurts.
Anji remembers his laugh as he sat on top of sandcastles.
She remembers when they thought he had gone back to the Big Sea. She remembers when Marasova watched them make snow turtles and when they looked after him when he was ill and bought polish and chocolate cakes. He helped Peter get in the school football team. He helped her with her spellings.
Anji thinks she can hear Marasova talking to her now. But all Anji can really hear are the gulls high in the sky and Peter's breathing.
Anji gives Peter a hug.
Then Peter kneels down and picks up two shells. One shell is blue and one shell is pink.
'It's like . . . it's like Marasova left us a present,' he says.
Anji looks at the shells and remembers how they painted them different colours.
'We must go home and tell Mum and Dad,' she says. 'And . . . and I want to write a letter and tell Marasova about my pink wellies.'

'And I want to tell Marasova about my certificate,' Peter says.

Anji nods and hugs Peter again.

Then they turn and walk slowly back towards the cliff steps.

TIP

This next activity is designed to be an opportunity for children to start processing what the story is about. Go straight on to it without a break after finishing the story.

■ Say,

> The feelings on the board are feelings Anji and Peter might have felt after Marasova died. Remember the ground rules each week? We are all different and Anji and Peter might feel all of the feelings or just some of them.

■ Think of one feeling the children might be feeling now. Stand up and tell a friend which one you have chosen.

TIP

Moving round will relieve tension. If some children are crying, reassure them that this is okay because the story is sad. Then encourage them to join in the activity.

■ Ask,

> What do you think someone who did not know Marasova might feel about him dying?

TIP

Refer back to the ground rules if need be; everyone reacts differently.

■ Ask children what we might do to help if someone who is important to one of our friends dies. Read out some of the list below and see what children think about each idea.

TIP

Some of these are deliberately slightly off the wall to relieve tension through laughter.

1 Be a good friend (explore what this means and refer back to the ground rules of listening and not having to share things that are too private).

2 Share some sweets with them.

3 Cry with them.

4 Listen carefully to what they are saying.

5 If you don't feel sad, that is okay.

TIP

Pretending is not helpful. Someone who is bereaved needs people to be honest.

6 Let them sit next to you.

7 If you are not the person's best friend, don't suddenly pretend you are.

8 Remember they might be feeling very sad.

9 Watch a DVD with them.

10 Play a game with them and let them win.

11 Maybe go to the funeral with them if it feels right.

12 Go to a football match with them.

13 Talk to them about the person who has died.

14 Hang out with them like you usually do.

15 Do something with them and include a few other people as well.

- Say,

  > When someone has a birthday we send cards so they know we are thinking about them. We do the same if someone dies. We're going to make a card for Peter and Anji. Hand out paper and let children design a card. Put the words Anji, Peter and Marasova on the board. This is a time to chat to children as they draw.

TIP

If asked about funerals, explain that it is a special ceremony to say 'good-bye' to someone who has died. People do different things, depending on what they believe, whether they have a religious faith, or believe a person goes to an afterlife when they die.

- Say,

  > Today we've thought about what we can do to help someone who is very, very ill. Not everyone who is ill gets better. We've also thought about how we might feel if someone dies and how we might help a friend after someone important to them dies.

TIP

The activity may have stirred up difficult feelings in some children so it is essential to reassure all the class and remind those who feel they need it where to go for support.

- Say,

  > All life has a beginning and an ending. Most people die when they are old but sadly some die when they are young. It is okay to talk about people who have died, or who are dying. Remember, in school there are people who will listen to you if there is anything you want to talk about, no matter what it is.

- On paper or whiteboards, let children draw anything they want to.

For children in early years or with learning difficulties

1 INTRODUCING THE BEACH, THE CHILDREN AND THE TURTLE

Children think about special places and people, feelings and wishes they make. Throughout, the term 'children' refers to those listening to and interacting with the story. The children in the text are referred to as Peter and Anji.

Preparation

Download pictures of (in this order) . . . a deserted beach, steps leading down a cliff face to a beach, a blue and yellow blow-up dinghy with oars, a seagull, a turtle, a storm, a chocolate cupcake (if possible with a birthday candle on it).

1   Read the first part of the story in one of the other versions so you know what happens in the story. Text is given to sequence the story. Add further details as appropriate.

2   Photocopy all the characters used in the story (see page 142 in Appendix B). Colour, cut out and fold them so they stand up. The children wear different clothes for different activities. If appropriate, children could be given their own set of characters.

3   Make the boat as shown on page 139 in Appendix A.

4   Think about how to make the beach setting. Below is how the one used when piloting the book was created. It took about ten minutes to make once everything needed had been found. When trialling the material, we used the box every week with younger children. In Year 4, it was used with an individual child who has Down's syndrome and in Year 3, with a group of children with learning difficulties. The Learning Support Assistants found the box really helped.

How to make the beach

Carefully pull out one of the long sides of a **shoe box** to create the front section which will become the sea (see Figure 2.1). Make sure this can be returned to its original position to reseal the box and keep the sand in it.

Use **cloth tape** (because it is very strong and very sticky) to seal the corners and the three internal edges. Masking tape and Sellotape are not as good as cloth tape for stopping sand leaking out of the box.

FIGURE 2.1 Open the shoe box and secure the edges with tape

Cut a **piece of A3 paper** lengthways and lay it round the inside of the box to make the white cliffs. The strip needs to be the height of the box plus three centimetres for the fence. In pencil, lightly mark on where the top of the steps will be drawn – they need to be level with the top of the box. Then take the strip out of the box and draw on the fence in **felt tipped pen** and cut out the gate. Add the steps and put the background back in the box. Use Blu-tack to secure it. Do not glue it as the cliffs will be removed to pack up the box.

Lay **clear plastic** on the bottom of the shoe box and cover with **four handfuls of dry sand** (builders' or sandpit play sand works well) (see Figure 2.2).

FIGURE 2.2 Add the background and sand

Lay strips of **green/blue tissue paper** over the front section to make the sea. Add **shells** and **pebbles**, **seagulls** and other beach things such as a doll's house-sized bucket and spade (see Figure 2.3). If no play boat is available, make the boat found on page 139 in Appendix A and also cut out the shed and house (Figures A.2 and A.4 on pages 138 and 140 in Appendix A).

Put the box lid behind the backdrop and stick the house in place (this can be permanent). The seagull moves in the story so attach it to the box lid with Blu-tack. Slot the shed in the sand.

Make the characters for lesson one but do not add them or Marasova until children have recapped beach vocabulary.

Marasova turtle can be made out of play dough or cut out (see page 142 in Appendix B); alternatively, type 'sea creature buttons' into an internet search engine.

FIGURE 2.3 Add the house, shed, strip characters, sea etc.

A world of interesting beach buttons appears, including perfectly sized dull greeny-grey turtles, seashells and gulls. The buttons are worth investing in as children can then physically bury Marasova in the sand at the end.

When the box is not in use, lift out the cliff backdrop, sea and anything else that is paper and lay it on the sand. Slot the flaps that house the sea back in place to remake the box and put the lid back on. Keep the box as flat as possible.

With the children . . .

- Explain that this story is about feelings.

- To help children feel safe, certain ground rules need to be talked about.

  1 You don't have to share something if you feel it is too private.
  2 Listen carefully to each other.
  3 We all have feelings and we are all different so it is okay not to feel the same as other people do.

110

- Look at pictures of an empty beach, cliffs with steps and a dinghy with oars and ask children what else you might find on a beach.

- Introduce the shoe box beach and focus on the vocabulary. Include the shed, gulls, rowing boat, sand, shells, steps, Peter and Anji's house.

- Using the characters and the beach, act out the story.

Peter and Anji play on the beach at the bottom of their garden.
They have a boat they love to go in.

- Talk about other things they might do on the beach.

One day Dad and Peter paint a blue football post on the cliffs. The lines are very wobbly.
Draw this on the back drop to the right of the cliff steps.
Anji and Peter love the beach.
It is their favourite place.

- Ask children about their favourite places and who they like to go there with. How do they feel when they are there?

- If appropriate, children could draw them.

Marasova turtle comes to live on the beach after a storm.
He is grey.
Marasova can talk and Anji and Peter understand what he says.
He becomes part of their family but still lives on the beach.
Anji and Peter often visit him.

- Use the characters in their fancy dress costumes.

Marasova has a birthday party on the beach.
Anji and Peter dress up for it.

■ Ask children what they would do at a party if it was on the beach.

Marasova has a chocolate birthday cake with six candles on.
'Make a wish!' Anji and Peter say when Marasova blows out the candles.
Marasova wishes he was bright yellow.

TIP

Phrases and concepts that need careful wording or explanation are written so they can be used directly from the script. These are indicated by the word 'Ask' or 'Say' written on a line with the question or comment on the line below.

■ Ask,

What wishes have you ever made? Explore whether they came true.

A gull steals the cake.
Peter shouts at it.
The gull drops poo that nearly hits Peter's foot.
Peter is cross.

■ Ask how Marasova felt when the gull stole his cake.

■ Say,

Today we have thought about feelings and wishes. Sometimes we feel happy, sometimes sad and sometimes . . . *say other feelings mentioned during the lesson.* These are feelings everyone has. When we get older, we will still be learning about them. Wishes are important too; sometimes they come true and sometimes they don't.

■ Let children draw anything they like from the story so far. This is to give them time to start processing what has been thought about during the lesson.

2 FOOTBALL TEAMS, BUILDING SANDCASTLES AND LOSING MARASOVA

Children think about their response to things they cannot control. One possible response is anger. They then think how they might feel when someone important to them has gone.

Preparation

Download pictures of . . . building sandcastles, fighting the tide, life jackets and marker buoys. Add these to last week's pictures.

Read the second part in one of the other versions. Photocopy, colour, cut and fold the appropriate characters as found on page 143 in Appendix B.

Possibly provide sand and buckets and spades to make sandcastles.

Have pink, blue and yellow paint ready to draw and paint seashells and pebbles – draw these if the real thing is not available. Have a football ready to be Peter.

Bring in something that is special to you that you can pretend you once lost.

■ Remind children about the story last time using pictures and the shoe box beach.

■ To help children feel safe, certain ground rules need to be talked about.
1 You don't have to share something if you feel it is too private.
2 Listen carefully to each other.
3 We all have feelings and we are all different so it is okay not to feel the same as other people do.

■ Today we are thinking about how we feel when things happen that we cannot change – such as when it rains all day.

■ Tell the story using the characters to act it out.

Anji's favourite colour is pink.
Peter's favourite colour is blue.
Marasova's favourite colour is yellow.
They paint shells and pebbles their favourite colours.

■ Colour or paint the shells and pebbles in children's favourite colours, or carry on with the story.

They dig sandcastles together.
They play football as well.
Peter is not very good at football.
He cannot kick the ball in the goal and becomes very angry.
'Why can't I get the ball in?' he shouts.

■ Play football and keep missing the goal like Peter did and pretend to be angry. Explain that Peter wants to change and become good at kicking the ball. He wants to get better but at the moment he cannot do it.

■ Explore when children are like Peter and become angry.

■ Continue acting out the story, using the folded character strips with the children wearing life jackets, found on page 143 in Appendix B.

Peter and Anji row their boat out to sea.
Marasova goes with them.
He drops off the front of the boat to go for a swim.
The children cannot see him.
They think he has gone and they have lost him.
Anji and Peter are worried and upset.
They row back to the beach.
When they get there, they pull the boat up the beach.
They are very sad.
But then they see Marasova swimming towards the beach.
'We thought we had lost you!' Anji says.

'No. I just went for a swim,' Marasova says.
They are so pleased to see him again.

- Show children the object you once lost. Tell them about how you felt and include 'scared' and 'helpless' and why you felt that.

- Ask,

    When have you lost something that was really special? How did it feel?

- Ask children to draw something they lost.

> **TIP**
>
> If children cannot think what to draw, let them draw the object you brought in.

- Say,

    Today we have thought about how things happen that we cannot change. It might make us feel angry. It could also make us feel scared and helpless, especially if something or someone who is really important goes missing.

3 SEVEN DAYS AND THEN MARASOVA IS PAINTED

Children think about grandparents, when someone is ill, and the importance of memories.

Preparation

Download pictures of home-made biscuits. Add these to previous pictures. Read the third part of the story in one of the other versions and photocopy the appropriate characters found on page 144 in Appendix B. Find dressing up clothes for someone who is ill and a blanket and pillow for an 'ill' child to lie on. Have torches ready for children to shine.

- To help children feel safe, certain ground rules need to be talked about.

  1 You don't have to share something if you feel it is too private.
  2 Listen carefully to each other.
  3 We all have feelings and we are all different and it is okay not to feel the same as other people do.

- Recap the story by looking at previous pictures and then at the biscuits. Today we are thinking about our grandparents and what happens when someone is ill.

- Take out the shoe box beach and remind children what is on/in it. Then tell the first part of today's story.

Peter and Anji like visiting their grandmother.
They make biscuits with Granny.
They always paint shells and pebbles and take them to give to her.

- Ask children what their grandparents do with them.

TIP

If children have never known grandparents, let them talk about things they have done with another relative or family friend. If children talk about grandparents who have died, let them share what they are comfortable sharing.

They miss their grandfather who died two years ago.
They miss the sound of his motorbike.
They miss playing games with him.
Granny talks to his picture.

- Highlight how children have lovely memories of their grandparents. After their grandparents have died, these will become really important. No one can ever take memories away. They will always be there to treasure.

■ Ask children if they have a grandparent who . . . loves them . . . wears fluffy slippers . . . has a beard . . . likes eating tomato soup. Then read the next part of the story.

One day Anji and Peter go to the beach and Marasova is ill.
He is ill for a whole week.
The children are very worried.
Very carefully, they carry him back home.
They make a special bed for him in their shed.
This is what they do while he is ill.
They go swimming and Peter plays football.
Chelsea lose and Dad cooks a curry.
On Saturday, Marasova says he feels better.
That is the best thing that happens all week.

■ Create a bed and ask a child to pretend he/she is ill. Think of one thing the children do each day. Talk about it while the child continues pretending to be ill.

■ On whiteboards or paper, ask children to draw one thing that happens in their homes when someone is ill.

■ Ask,

> How do you feel if someone is ill for a long time?

TIP

Let the children know that it is okay to feel grumpy and find it difficult if someone is ill for a long time.

When Marasova is better Anji and Peter take him back to the beach.
They want to cheer him up.
So they tiptoe down to the beach in the middle of the night.
Peter holds the torch because it is dark.

- Let children hold torches and close their eyes to imagine what it might have been like in the dark.

- Talk about what Peter and Anji are wearing.

> **TIP**
>
> Elaborate on pyjamas and nighties having interesting motifs and patterns, such as frogs and football club badges.

They take bright yellow paint with them.
Marasova is asleep.
Anji and Peter paint his grey shell so it becomes bright yellow.
Marasova loves his new colour.
'Thank you,' he says to the children.

> **TIP**
>
> NB – in other versions of the story, Anji feels guilty. The concept of 'guilt' is not explored in this version.

A few weeks later, it snows. Anji and Peter build a snow turtle (or snowman) on the beach.
They throw snowballs at each other.
Peter and Anji think they will remember the day forever.

- What have children done that they think they will remember?

- Say,

> What we remember about people is really important. We have thought about what it's like when someone is seriously ill; it can be difficult for everyone and it is okay to find it difficult.

- Let children draw as they begin to process their thoughts.

4 CARING FOR EACH OTHER WHEN SOMEONE DIES

Children think about how we might support each other and people who are very ill and how we night feel after someone we know dies.

Preparation

Be aware of any children who have recently been bereaved. Read the last part in one of the other versions. Photocopy the characters on page 145 in Appendix B.

Find pictures of people who help ill people – such as doctors, nurses, family, friends, ambulance drivers.

■ Revisit the ground rules.

1 Children don't have to share something if they feel it is too private.
2 Listen carefully to each other.
3 We have talked about lots of feelings. If someone dies, some people feel very sad and other people might not feel anything at all. We're all different and it is okay not to feel the same as other people do.

TIP

Recapping the third rule is especially important today.

■ Recap the story by asking children what happened.

■ Today we are thinking about how people might support each other when someone is hurting.

TIP

In order to keep this lesson objective, when working with the whole class, avoid sharing personal experiences.

- Make a list of feelings talked about so far while thinking about Peter, Anji and Marasova on the beach.

- Record the list, either in words, by drawing facial expressions or using symbols.

- Tell the next part of the story using the characters to act it out.

The children think Marasova needs a house.
So they take Anji's doll's house to the beach.
The gulls keep flying really close to the doll's house.
One of them flies into the house and injures herself.
Marasova is kind and looks after the gull until she is better.
The other gulls are sorry they were nasty to Marasova earlier on.

- Say,

    Last week we talked about what it might be like at home when someone is ill. When Marasova was ill, Anji and Peter tried to cheer him up by painting his shell bright yellow.

    The gull's wing is mending but can you think about what it is like for someone who is not just a bit ill, but very, very ill for a long time and is not getting better?

- Ask,

    What do people who are very ill do and what don't they not do?

TIP

Keep this light – e.g., they don't go sand dancing or run the marathon. Lighter moments help children feel they are more in control of the lesson content. They do stay in bed, don't want to eat and even watching the telly can be too much.

■ Draw a picture in the middle of the large sheet of paper of someone who is ill in bed. Then stick pictures (or draw) and label all the people who might be able to help that person.

TIP

Make sure 'friends' are mentioned.

■ When children say doctors and nurses, say,

> They make people better but sometimes people are so ill they cannot be made better because they are too ill for the medicines to work.

■ Read the next part of the story.

One morning the children go to the beach.

Marasova's body is cold and still.

He has died.

His body is there but he cannot talk to them or smile or eat or laugh or swim.

Anji and Peter cry and feel very sad.

They remember the things they have done with Marasova.

They played football, painted shells and pebbles, ate chocolate cake, rowed in the boat, built sandcastles.

They go home and tell Mum and Dad.

Later, they return to the beach to say 'good-bye' to him.

They bury him in the sand.

Both of them draw a picture to say 'thank you' for the friendship and love he has given them.

TIP

This next activity is designed to be an opportunity for children to start processing what the story is about. Go straight on to it without a break after finishing the story.

■ Say,

> Over the last few weeks, the feelings we have thought about are feelings Anji and Peter might have when Marasova has died. Anji and Peter might feel all of the feelings or just some of them or none of them.

■ Ask children to think of some of the feelings Anji and Peter might be feeling right now when they have just found out that Marasova is dead. There are no right or wrong answers.

They can stand up and share their chosen feelings with a friend.

TIP

Moving round will relieve tension. If some children are crying, reassure them that this is okay because the story is sad.

■ Think of things we might do to help if one of our friends had someone important to them die.

TIP

Refer back to the ground rules if need be; everyone reacts differently.

■ Include these things . . .

1 Be a good friend (explore what this means – refer back to the ground rules of listening and not having to share things that are too private).

2 Invite them round to play.

3 Be kind to them.

4 Listen carefully to what they are saying.

5 If you don't feel sad, that is okay.

TIP

Pretending is not helpful. Someone who is bereaved needs people to be honest.

6   Treat your friend normally but remember they might be feeling a bit wobbly and sad at times.

- Say,

    If it is someone's birthday we send cards to let them know we are thinking about them. We do the same if someone dies. We're going to design a card to Peter and Anji to let them know we are thinking about them.

- Hand out paper so children can make a card for Anji and Peter. This is a time to chat to children as they draw.

TIP

If asked about funerals, explain that it is a special ceremony to say 'good-bye' to someone who has died. People do different things, depending on what they believe, whether they have a religious faith or believe a person goes to heaven after they die.

- Say,

    Today we've thought about what we and other people might do to help someone who is very, very ill. Sadly, not everyone who is ill gets better because sometimes they are too ill for medicines to work. We've thought about what we might feel after someone dies and how we might help a friend after someone important to them has died.

    All life has a beginning and an ending; it is all part of the life cycle. Most people die when they are old but sadly some die when they are young. It is OK to talk about people who have died, or who are dying. Remember, in school there are people who will listen to you if there is anything you want to talk about, no matter what it is.

- On paper or whiteboards, let children draw anything they want to.

Using the story to support a bereaved child

This book's original intent is to help children learn about loss, death and grief before they have to face it. However, it can also be used as a support resource with a grieving child, or children, after someone important to them has died.

Teachers are not bereavement counsellors and should not be expected to take on that role, but Child Bereavement UK has learned from the children they work with that what children value is spending time with a trusted adult who cares about them. The story creates an ideal opportunity to do this.

Select an appropriate version for the age of the child and familiarise yourself with the story and the activities by reading it through carefully. Use the story in any way that feels right. What matters is creating time and space for a pupil to express feelings and talk about the person who has died, should they want to. Just reading the story with you will for some children be all that they need. When the time feels right, you can introduce some of the activities. Let the child set the pace and the focus.

FROM THE AUTHOR – HOW I UNEXPECTEDLY HAD TO USE THE STORY IN REAL LIFE

Very sadly, the father of one of the children in my class suddenly died. This was the class that, only three weeks before, I had used to trial the story. The father who died was well known to the school and some of my pupils. This is how I used the material with the class.

I started by asking the class whether they could remember the ground rules used at the beginning of each lesson on Marasova. The bereaved child was not present. We then went through each one. This resulted in the following discussion.

We talked about how they would all be feeling different things and that each would have a different memory of the Dad who died. We then shared the memories. I think this helped children realise they were not alone, that others also liked him and it was okay to talk openly about someone who had died. For several of the children, the situation brought back memories of grandparents who had died. I reminded them that it helps to talk but only if they want to. Talking can be a way to look after yourself and we all need to do that now.

I reminded them that the classmate whose Dad had died would have times when he might want to talk about what had happened, and times when he wouldn't. This might also apply to those in the class who knew the Dad. As good friends we would give them the space to do that.

We also talked about how it is natural to want to know what had happened but we need to think carefully before asking our classmate any questions. I suggested that if there was anything they wanted to know that they ask me.

We talked about how there would be times when their classmate might cry. I reminded them that to feel like crying after someone has died is natural, but it is also okay not to. Some of us will be very sad, and others will not, but as a class we can still share in what has happened simply by being good friends to one another.

I then asked the class how they thought their bereaved friend might be feeling and they came up with a list that included . . . ballistic, incandescent with rage, depressed, unbubbly, tearful, heartbroken, shy, black-hearted, upset, emotionless, angry because other people will get cross and angry about silly things, dull, furious, lonely, sorrow, frustrated, frightened, alone, shattered, moody, tired, grumpy, small in a big world.

I reminded the class where some of these feelings appeared in the story. This reminded the children of some of the funny pictures they had drawn. The resultant laughter was a helpful tension reliever.

I asked the children to share with a partner any of those feelings they were currently experiencing and reminded them that it was okay not to have any of these feelings.

We then thought about how they might be able to help their friend. We agreed together to carry on as normal but also understand that there would be times when he might show how sad he was by crying or perhaps just being very quiet. At those times we would let him do what he felt he needed to do but without crowding round him. I reminded everyone that grief doesn't go away and that there will always be times when he might be feeling sad.

125

GROUNDING ACTIVITY

We did some exercises on the spot and made animal noises. This was to relieve any tensions.

The class then made cards which I later took round to the family. This made a natural entry point to reassure about how school could support them. I also gave them details of Child Bereavement UK.

Further information and resources

Child Bereavement UK
REBUILDING LIVES TOGETHER

www.childbereavementuk.org
Tel 01494 568900

HOW CHILDREN AND YOUNG PEOPLE GRIEVE

As concerned adults, we would like to be reassured that children are too young to feel the deep sadness and despair that grief can bring. Sadly, this is not the case. Children and young people grieve just as deeply as adults but they show it in different ways. They learn how to grieve by mirroring the responses of the adults around them, and rely on adults to provide them with what they need to support them in their grief.

Common responses, feelings and behaviours

Children have a limited ability to put feelings, thoughts and memories into words and tend to 'act out' with behaviours rather than express themselves verbally.

Children are naturally good at dipping in and out of their grief. They can be intensely sad one minute, then suddenly switch to playing happily the next. This apparent lack of sadness may lead adults to believe children are unaffected, but this 'puddle jumping' is a type of in-built safety mechanism that prevents them being overwhelmed by powerful feelings. As children get older, this instinctive 'puddle 'jumping' becomes harder and teenagers may spend long periods of time in one behaviour or another.

It is normal for children and young people to react strongly to the death of someone close even if the resulting feelings and behaviours look and feel far from normal. You may notice some of the following, which are all okay as long as they do not go on for too long:

- Change in behaviour, perhaps becoming unnaturally quiet and withdrawn or unusually aggressive. Anger is a common response at all ages and may be directed at people or events that have no connection to the death.
- Disturbed sleep and bad dreams.
- Anxiety demonstrated by clinging behaviour and a reluctance to be separated from parents or carers. Older children may express this in more practical ways, with concerns over issues that adults may perceive as insensitive, such as lifts to activities.
- Being easily upset by events that would normally be trivial.
- Difficulty concentrating, being forgetful and generally 'not with it'. This makes school work particularly hard and academic performance may suffer. Older children may feel that there is no point in working hard at school and might lose a general sense of purpose in their lives.
- Physical complaints, such as headaches, stomach aches and a general tendency to be run down and prone to minor illness.

AGE AND UNDERSTANDING

All children are different and a mature 4-year-old may have a better grasp of the situation, and of the full meaning of what being dead means, than a child who is older.

Toddler to 5 years of age

Children of this age find it hard to grasp the permanence of death and can have an expectation of the person returning. They may struggle with the concept of 'no life' and therefore need reassurance that dead people feel nothing and are not in pain. Anxieties about everyday practicalities are common as is increased separation anxiety even when left for short periods. There may be a regression in behaviour, for example with bed wetting, and generally behaving like a younger child.

Primary school age

Children of this age are beginning to grasp the concept that dead people do not return to life and that death happens to everyone, including themselves. They can start to fear the death of others important to them. Some children react by being especially good to compensate for a sense of badness that somehow what has happened was their fault. Others behave badly to attract the punishment that they feel they deserve. Even when there is no expectation, they sometimes take on the role of carer for a surviving adult or siblings, and in an attempt to appear grown-up they sometimes take on inappropriate adult responsibilities.

Secondary school age

Puberty is a time of great change and for a young person grief just adds to this. Teenagers are striving to be independent and grown-up but the death of someone close creates vulnerability. Their feelings of grief may be similar to those of adults but they have strong inhibitions about expressing them, partly to be grown-up, and partly to avoid being different from their friends. Some young people become apathetic, depressed and withdrawn and develop a 'what's the point' attitude to school or even life. A hectic social life prevents time to think and risk-taking behaviour or antisocial behaviour is not unusual.

None of the above is a cause for concern unless it lasts a long time or affects a child's or a young person's ability to engage with normal life. If you are unsure or concerned, you can call the Child Bereavement UK Support and Information line on 01494 568900 for guidance. It is important to remember that grief is normal and, with the right help and support, most children and young people will be changed, but not damaged, by what has happened.

HOW SCHOOLS CAN HELP

Most grieving pupils do not need a 'bereavement expert'. They need people who care. Schools, just by carrying on with their usual day-to-day activities, can do a huge amount to support a grieving child. The following are some helpful things schools can offer children and young people experiencing loss and grief.

Normality

For a child or young person whose life has been turned upside down, the routines of school life can give a sense of normality. Everything else may have fallen apart but school and the people within it are still there, offering a sense of security and continuity.

Relief from grief

For young children and adolescents, school can give relief from an emotionally charged atmosphere at home. They may feel overwhelmed by a grieving family. There may be a constant stream of visitors expressing their own grief. Children and young people can find this difficult to deal with.

An outlet for grief

When a parent or sibling has died, children and young people can try to spare their surviving parent by hiding their own grief and appearing to be okay. School is often seen as somewhere safe to express this grief.

A listening ear

Children can be overlooked by family members struggling to deal with their own grief. For a child who wishes to, school staff can provide an opportunity to talk about what has happened with a familiar and trusted adult in relative peace and calm.

The opportunity to be a child

Even when deeply sad, children still need to be children. Loss and grief are very grown-up experiences. School offers the chance to play, laugh, sing and generally just be a child without feeling guilty.

General support

Keep in contact with home. Discuss concerns, but equally important are successes. The family or carers will find this reassuring. Grieving children and young people can display altered behaviours in different situations. Good communication with home will help the school be aware of this and provide a more realistic picture of how the child is coping.

Resources

Have in school a selection of resources on the subject. Refer to the recommended books on pages 132–135. Stories are a wonderful way to gently introduce young children to the concept of death.

HELPFUL ORGANISATIONS

Child Bereavement UK: www.childbereavementuk.org
Support and Information Line 01494 568900.

Child Bereavement UK supports families and educates professionals both when a baby or child dies or is dying, and when a child is bereaved. Families and professionals can call the support line to receive information, guidance and signposting to other organisations. It has a comprehensive website, with a section containing a wealth of information for schools including a short film *What Teachers Need To Know* and lesson plans for PSHE. The training programme has a wide selection of courses and workshops, several of which are specifically designed for schools. There is also information for young people. Publications can be bought online, and articles and leaflets downloaded for free. A discussion forum for families provides online support.

Winston's Wish: www.winstonswish.org.uk

This charity offers a well-produced range of resources and publications. The inter- active website has a special section for young people where they can email questions to a bereavement counsellor and share experiences with other bereaved children. Teachers should view it before recommending to a child.

Brake: www.brake.org.uk

A road safety charity that offers emotional support and practical information to anyone bereaved, or seriously injured, in a road crash. An excellent booklet for children 'Someone Has Died in a Road Crash' can be downloaded for free.

Cruse Bereavement Care: www.rd4u.org.uk

Run by Cruse for bereaved children and young people, a site that offers news, information and a monitored message board. Teachers should view it before recom- mending to a child.

For information on further organisations in different locations across the UK see the Child Bereavement UK searchable database: www.childbereavement.org.uk/ Support/OtherSupportOrganisations.

RESOURCES FOR STAFF

The Little Book of Bereavement for Schools by Ian Gilbert and his children aged 9, 13 and 18

A short, personal account of how educational establishments responded after a mother's death. It has a fifteen-point, straightforward guide for any school wondering what to do after the death of a parent. Published by Crown House.

Childhood Bereavement: Developing the curriculum and pastoral support by Nina Job and Gill Francis

Using case studies, this useful resource aims to help those working in schools address death, dying and bereavement from both a pastoral care and educational perspective. Available from The National Children's Bureau: Tel: 020 7843 6029.

Working with Bereaved Children and Young People by Brenda Mallon

A wide-ranging and helpful resource with a focus on practical skills. Includes a section on a whole school approach to bereavement. Sage Publications.

Then, Now and Always by J. Stokes

Suitable for those with pastoral care responsibilities, this guide for supporting children as they journey through grief includes a section on enabling a school community to respond positively to a death. Published by and available from Winston's Wish: www.winstonswish.org.uk.

When Someone Very Special Dies by M. Heegard

A simple workbook designed to be used by a bereaved child with adult help. Communication and coping skills are developed. Available from Amazon.

'What Teachers Need to Know" and 'A Message to Parents'

Short video clips that are excellent for training purposes or staffroom discussion. Can be viewed at www.childbereavement.org.uk/Support/Youngpeople.

RESOURCES FOR PARENTS/CARERS

When your Partner Dies: Supporting your children

Written with help from bereaved families, this simple booklet offers information and guidance for surviving parents and carers. Available from Child Bereavement UK.

A Child's Grief

This is a short book for any adult supporting a bereaved child. It covers lots of issues and offers practical suggestions and activities. From Winston's Wish: www.winstonswish.org.uk.

BOOKS FOR CHILDREN IN EARLY YEARS

I Miss You: A first look at death by **Pat Thomas**

This helps children understand that death is a natural complement to life, and that grief and a sense of loss are normal feelings. It is a good one to use to introduce the subject.

Granpa by **John Burningham**

This award-winning book is a beautifully written tale about the close and imaginative relationship between a little girl and her Granpa. The last page is an illustration of Granpa's empty chair with the little girl beside it looking very thoughtful.

Someone I Know Has Died by **Trish Phillips**

This activity book is designed to be used with very young children who need help to understand what being dead means, what we do and how we might feel when someone dies. Some pages are interactive in ways familiar to young children. To be used with an adult; guidance notes are included. Available from Child Bereavement UK www.childbereavementuk.org/shop.

BOOKS FOR CHILDREN IN KS1 AND KS2

Badger's Parting Gifts (also available in Urdu and Arabic) by Susan Varley

When old Badger dies, his friends think they will be sad forever. But gradually they start to remember Badger with joy and to treasure the gifts he left behind for every one of his friends. Published by Collins Picture Lions.

I Miss My Sister by Sarah Courtauld

A young girl's sister has died. The impact on her and her family is sensitively illustrated with minimum text. Designed to be shared with an adult, this book should help start conversations, and answer questions. Available from Child Bereavement UK www.childbereavementuk.org/shop, for use with children aged 4–10 but could be used with younger children.

My Brother and Me by Sarah Courtauld

This pre-bereavement book is designed to help children understand how they and the rest of their family might feel when someone in that family is seriously ill. Suitable for age 4–10 but could be used with younger children. It is available from Child Bereavement UK www.childbereavementuk.org/shop.

Beginnings and Endings with Lifetimes in Between by Bryan Mellonie and Robert Ingpen

A beautifully illustrated book that aims to help parents and teachers explore the subjects of life and death with young children.

Remembering by Dianne Leutner

This is a keepsake book. Sensitively illustrated, it will help a child talk about their memories and make some sense of how they are feeling. Only available from Child Bereavement UK www.childbereavementuk.org/shop.

BOOKS FOR CHILDREN WITH LEARNING DIFFICULTIES

When Someone Very Special Dies by Marge Heegard

A simple workbook that could be adapted for use with SEN children and young people. With adult help, users are invited to illustrate and personalise their loss. It also encourages the identification of support systems and personal strengths. Available from Amazon.

Hand-in-Hand

A resource pack for schools with practical ideas for supporting children and young people with learning difficulties through the experience of bereavement. It includes a section on using symbols to explain death and funerals. Produced by and available from SeeSaw: Tel 01865 744768.

To make the beach

> **NOTE**
>
> To reproduce these scenes at the intended size, please set the copy ratio of your photocopier to 140 per cent

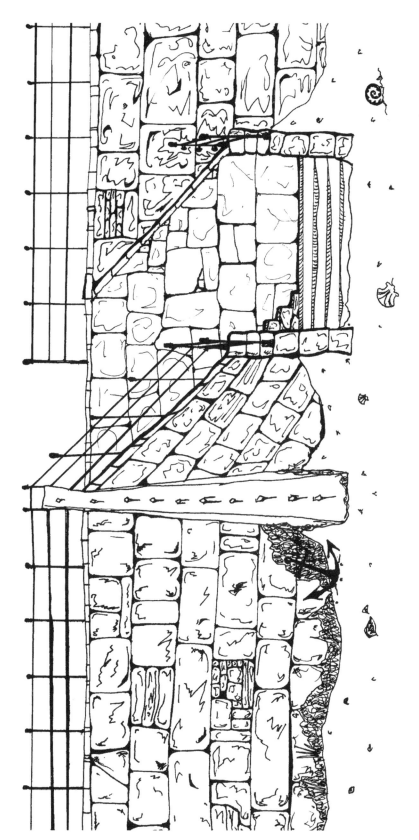

FIGURE A.1 Beachhead background

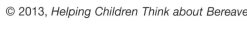

FIGURE A.2 Background house

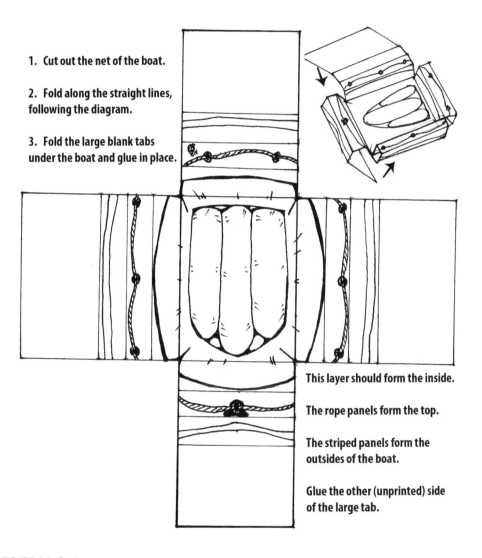

1. Cut out the net of the boat.

2. Fold along the straight lines, following the diagram.

3. Fold the large blank tabs under the boat and glue in place.

This layer should form the inside.

The rope panels form the top.

The striped panels form the outsides of the boat.

Glue the other (unprinted) side of the large tab.

FIGURE A.3 Boat

If you cut along one side and the top of the door you can place the characters in the shed

FIGURE A.4 Shed

Strip characters of Peter and Anji

NOTE

To reproduce the characters on the following pages at the intended size, please set the copy ratio of your photocopier to 140 per cent

LESSON 1

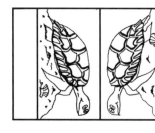
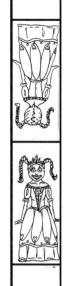

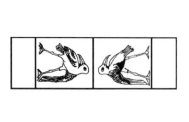

LESSON 2

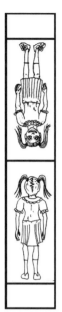
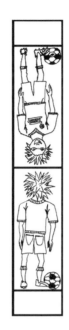
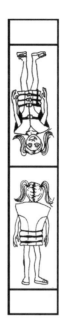
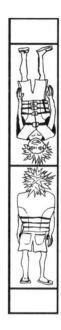

LESSON 3

  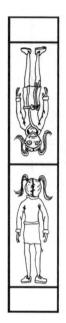 

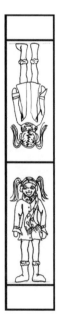 

LESSON 4

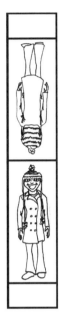
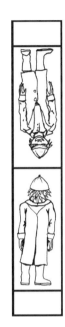

Index